CHANNELS (Hungary)

The Stonewatcher
(A Gézagyerek)

by János Háy
translated by Phil Porter
from a literal translation by László Bíró and László Upor

The Stonewatcher was first read in the UK, in this
translation, at the Cottesloe Theatre on 17 June 2004.

The reading was directed by Anna Mackmin.

T0347803

CHANNELS

By Philippe Le Moine, International Projects Manager NT Studio

One of the National Theatre Studio's flagship initiatives, *CHANNELS* aims to instigate and nurture a direct creative exchange between the vibrant, but somewhat insular, world of British theatre and its corresponding foreign counterparts.

A programme with ever-expanding horizons, each *CHANNELS* project strives to bring together writers, translators and directors from the UK and one specific country, with a view to translating and presenting a selection of current British plays abroad, and foreign works at the National and beyond.

At the heart of the project lies a process of hand-in-hand interaction, with the playwright and translator taking a literal translation as their starting point and building a mutual understanding of one another's methods and ideas. These 'residencies' are the cornerstone of a scheme infused with discovery and exchange.

Five French plays were translated, read at the National Theatre and published by Oberon Books in 2002. *Channels (Hungary)* is the second project and runs alongside *Channels (Argentina)*. Quebec and The Czech Republic are also on the cards.

Following the heartening success of *CHANNELS*, a network of like-minded organisations has emerged. INTERTEXT covers major partner languages: French, German and Italian, and carries forward the spirit of *CHANNELS* as a permanent European platform for translation and encounters.

For more information on the NT Studio's International projects:
studio@nationaltheatre.org.uk

NT Studio

Head of Studio	LUCY DAVIES
International Projects Manager	PHILIPPE LE MOINE
Studio Manager	NATASHA BUCKNOR
Technical Manager	EDDIE KEOGH
Studio Administrator	RACHEL LONERGAN
Studio Assistant	MATTHEW POXON
Book Keeper	VERA PROLE
Reception	CATHY MILLER, JANLYN BALES
Security Officer	LLOYD WILDMAN

NT Literary Department

Literary Manager	JACK BRADLEY
Assistant Literary Manager	LAURA GRIBBLE
Senior Reader	CHRIS CAMPBELL
Scripts Assistant	SARAH CLARKE

CHANNELS (Hungary)

by Katalin Trencsényi

When I was a teenager I came across an interesting riddle about reading. It concerned two brothers who were trying to read a book. One of them could recognise the letters and read aloud the words without understanding the meaning, whereas the other could understand the meaning, but could not interpret the letters. So they decided to work together. The one who knew the letters spelt them out, and the other explained the meaning of the words. The question was: which of them was reading? The answer was neither of them. Both of these skills are needed in order to read a text.

This story occurred to me several times whilst working with the British playwrights on their English translations of these four plays for the *Channels (Hungary)* project. Sometimes it seemed as if we were trying to make the impossible possible. How could we two translators – one who could not read the play in its original language and one whose mother tongue wasn't English – work together on one piece?

We had the original play in Hungarian, and a literal translation with a number of added footnotes clarifying problematic areas. This formed the basis for several drafts which were worked and reworked to arrive at the final version of the translation.

Like the two brothers in the riddle we couldn't have done it without each other. We literal translators knew the language and the cultural background of the play – where the play 'came from'. Whereas our British playwright colleagues knew the language and the theatrical culture into which the play was heading.

During our one-week residency at the National Theatre Studio we 'twins' became 'triplets', as the Hungarian playwrights joined us to help with the translation. They answered questions we had about the plays, explained hidden meanings, tiny details and revealed their way of thinking and their working process. We went through the plays word-by-word, comparing the translations with the original, checking things like the social context, the rhythms of the phrases, and debating the precise meaning of certain words.

We had to answer such questions as: How many miles from Budapest is Irgács, the hidden village where Zoltán Egressy's play is set? Would a Hassidic Jew use the word synagogue? How should we distinguish formal and informal verb conjugations in English? What kind of drug are the gangsters dealing in Ákos Németh's play? What's the English equivalent for 'pálinka'?

As one of the playwrights, Péter Kárpáti recalled *"A painstaking but very exciting process now began: we were flying from word to word! ... Dennis [Kelly] enjoyed the excess and the 'garlic-spiced' humour of the Hungarian text – I enjoyed his elegance, the way he delicately sharpened the Hungarian sentences: in English they sound less ambiguous, more precise. I can hardly speak any English, he doesn't speak Hungarian, but strangely our intuitive sense of language enabled us to engage in an elaborate dialogue. Who can explain this?"*

Our work did not conclude with the end of the residency. We spent another five months finalising, checking, clarifying and double-checking the translations.

This isn't to say that using a single translator isn't effective, and often even preferable. But using multiple translators suited the nature of this project.

Aside from producing good English translations of the plays, the other aim of the project was to encourage the playwrights to exchange ideas and perhaps learn from each other; maybe in the process discovering new worlds, different ways of thinking, fresh working methods. Perhaps it also showed that regardless of where in this world a playwright is working he/she will face similar questions and problems. As a discussion during the residency revealed, whether Hungarian or English, it is impossible to find inspiration when writing with a blue biro!

The Stonewatcher by János Háy was first published as a short story, under the title of *Gézagyerek* (*Géza The Kid*). Later Háy developed four of these stories into a tetralogy for the stage. *The Stonewatcher* is the first play in this tetralogy. In each play in the tetralogy (*The Stonewatcher, Ferike Herner's Pa, The Senák, Uncle Pityu's Son*) Háy makes use of a different dramaturgy. *The Stonewatcher*, as the playwright notes, *"is a piece without action, which is 'oiled' by the central character."* This is Géza, a young man with learning difficulties.

The play is set in a village somewhere in Northern Hungary. The people it deals with live on the periphery of society – low-paid workers, alcoholics, benefit dependants.

There is a quarry not too far from the village which used to provide jobs for people living nearby. It was from the stones in this quarry that the country was built. These stones were used to construct the first motorway in Hungary and build the underground in Budapest. Following the political and economic changes of the early 1990s this state-owned quarry became unprofitable and had to be closed down. The villagers thus lost their principle means of income. However, a German businessman then bought the quarry and re-employed some of the villagers. The rest still live on benefits and regard with envy the privileged few who are employed (despite the fact that they earn hardly more than those on benefits).

The German owner is a kind of Godot-like figure. He never appears in the play and no-one ever sees him although he is often spoken about by the workers whose lives depend on him. The German is the one who sets things in motion. It's due to his new safety regulations that Géza is employed in the quarry.

Géza is the 'village fool', on the lowest rung of the social ladder. A young man with learning difficulties who has never before had the opportunity to work. So, when the boss of the quarry offers him a job he suddenly becomes the centre of attention. The job raises his status and he becomes a 'proper man' at last. The job entails overseeing the belt carrying the stones from the quarry, and stopping it in case of an emergency.

Géza believes in regulation and order and in his new position he identifies himself with God whose job it is to watch and govern the world, and also to mend its faults. However he gradually comes to realise that his job is in fact pointless, it makes no difference whether he's there or not.

Géza now understands that the regulation and order which he once accepted without question have become senseless and empty. However when he questions this order, the other workers – who have become desensitised by this inhuman regime – react by playing a cruel trick on Géza which almost destroys him and makes him more isolated than ever. The play ends with Géza, back where he started, in his corner in the kitchen, counting the stones on the floor.

Háy beautifully depicts these downtrodden characters – not without a little humour – and he portrays Géza's inner life with great skill and authenticity.

But Háy's greatest innovation is in the language of the play. He creates an almost Beckettian texture of repetitions, rhythms and pauses. He takes the worn out, misused, corrupted language of these people and weaves poetry out of it. Háy in this play has done nothing less than create a new dramatic language.

"With Géza the Kid *and the other three short stories I discovered a language which I felt I had to develop further,"* says Háy. *"It is essential that the language with which you seize the world must be alive for you [as a writer]. There are thousands of ways of knowing the world, but for a writer it is the language through which they are expressed which is important."*

All four of the plays in this anthology are new dramas written by the best contemporary Hungarian playwrights of the new generation. Tried, tested and awarded in Hungary and on the continent. The world they describe may be a little different, but you might find the people they introduce surprisingly familiar.

Special thanks to my husband Nick Tomalin, for his help with the translations and Vivienne Menkes-Ivry a great friend, for her wise advice and encouragement.

JÁNOS HÁY

János Háy is an award-winning poet, short-story writer and novelist with over fourteen books published. He started to write plays only a few years ago. In 1997 and 1998 he wrote the lyrics for two children's musicals (*The Salt* and *Briar Rose*), then between 2001 and 2004 wrote his tetralogy, the first of which was *The Stonewatcher*. It caused a stir in Hungarian theatre circles and won him several awards.

PHIL PORTER

Phil Porter's *Smashed Eggs*, a play for eight- to eleven-year-olds, was the winner of the Arts Council's 2003 Children's Play Award and was given a national tour. He is currently writing plays for the Bush Theatre, the Pentabus Theatre and the Unicorn Theatre. He was writer in residence at the Pentabus until July 2003. *Broken* was performed at the Edinburgh Fringe Festival and the Hen and Chickens Theatre in London in 1999/2000; and *Isolated Children in Far Away Places* was put on at the Royal Exchange Studio in Manchester in 2001. *Stealing Sweets and Punching People*, which was written as part of an attachment to the National Theatre Studio, has recently been published, and performed at the Latchmere Theatre in London.

LÁSZLÓ BÍRÓ

László Bíró studied English literature and linguistics at the ELTE University in Budapest. He is a freelance translator and interpreter, translating plays and prose for a number of different theatres and theatre projects in Hungary, as well as dubbing international films into Hungarian. He is currently writing a new play for a theatre company in Budapest, and also working as a dramaturg.

LÁSZLÓ UPOR

László Upor is an award-winning dramaturg and translator who since 2002 has been a dramaturg at the National Theatre in Budapest. He is also a lecturer in dramaturgy at the city's University of Drama and Film. As well as nurturing the future generation of Hungarian dramaturgs and playwrights, he is actively involved in gaining exposure in Hungary for contemporary foreign playwrights: he is the co-editor of a series of drama anthologies published by Európa and has edited a number of collections of contemporary British, Irish and American plays. He was also the editor of the collection *Hungarian Plays: New Drama from Hungary*, published by Nick Hern Books in 1996.

CHANNELS (Hungary) 2004
National Theatre, Cottesloe

Thursday 17 June, 2.30pm
THE STONEWATCHER
by János Háy
translated by Phil Porter
directed by Anna Mackmin

Friday 18 June, 2.30pm
THE FOURTH GATE
by Péter Kárpáti
translated by Dennis Kelly
directed by Alex Murdoch

Thursday 24 June, 2.30pm
CAR THIEVES
by Ákos Németh
translated by Ché Walker
directed by Ché Walker

Friday 25 June, 2.30pm
PORTUGAL
by Zoltán Egressy
translated by Ryan Craig
directed by Matt Wilde

MAGYAR MAGIC – Hungary in Focus 2004, a year-long celebration of Hungarian art and talent in the UK

by Katalin Bogyay, Director of the Hungarian Cultural Centre and Magyar Magic

Culture is us, it is democratic, it is about experiences and relationships. For me, culture is a framework for collective creativity.

I had a dream four years ago. To create a Hungarian Cultural Centre, a cultural space in London that would provide an important meeting-place where ideas, talent and experiences from both East and West could be exchanged in an inspirational and welcoming environment. Four years on, people and cultures from the Thames to the Danube have indeed come together in Maiden Lane to take part in our cultural exchange. A network of artists, writers, musicians and intellectuals has evolved organically, watched over by the spirits of the Vaudeville Theatre, which gives the HCC a home in Covent Garden. Our culture is welcoming and inclusive, facilitating creative links and finding meeting-points. These aspirations are symbolized by the Centre's Palladian window, which is always open.

Now, on the threshold of the New Europe, within the framework of Magyar Magic, we will share with you, in a very intense way, our thousand-year-old cultural heritage, which is full of unique, high-level but often lesser-known artistic values, and also full of glamour and good-tempered fun. Hungarian culture is a wonderful mixture of traditional, organic and contemporary elements.

As members of Europe, we are all in a position to absorb, peacefully and of our own free will, one another's cultural influences. And let us hope that out of this melting pot a New European style will emerge, which will in no way diminish the cultural identities of individual nations. I see Magyar Magic as the beginning of a new kind of cultural dialogue that will continue far into the future.

Thank you to everyone for believing in my vision of four years ago and for joining me on this journey.

Thanks are due to the Ministry of Cultural Heritage in Hungary for its support and its determination to see Hungarian Cultural Seasons launched all over Europe.

Thank you to my dedicated colleagues at the HCC, whose boundless energy, knowledge and team spirit have helped me to make this dream come true.

Thanks, too, go to our partners and friends here in the UK whom I proudly regard as 'Honorary Hungarians'.

This book is published as part of Magyar Magic – Hungary in Focus 2004, a year-long celebration of Hungarian art and talent in the United Kingdom supported by the Hungarian Ministry of Cultural Heritage.

www.magyarmagic.com

NEMZETI KULTURÁLIS ÖRÖKSÉG
MINISZTÉRIUMA

THE NATIONAL THEATRE

Chairman of the Board   Sir Christopher Hogg
Chairman Designate   Hayden Phillips
Director of the NT   Nicholas Hytner
Executive Director   Nick Starr

The National Theatre presents an eclectic mix of new plays and classics, with seven or eight productions in repertory at any one time. It aims constantly to re-energise the great traditions of the British stage and to expand the horizons of audiences and artists alike, and aspires to reflect in its repertoire the diversity of the culture. At its Studio, the National offers a space for research and development for the NT's stages and the theatre as a whole. Through the NT Education Department, tomorrow's audiences are addressed. Through an extensive programme of Platform performances, backstage tours, foyer music, exhibitions, and free outdoor entertainment the National recognises that the theatre doesn't begin and end with the rise and fall of the curtain.

NT Platforms are daytime and early-evening discussions, talks and interviews offering an insight into the National's current productions and showcasing theatre-related events.

National Theatre, South Bank, London SE1 9PX
www.nationaltheatre.org.uk
Registered Charity No: 224223

THE STONEWATCHER

First published in 2004 by Oberon Books Ltd
(Incorporating Absolute Classics.)
521 Caledonian Road, London N7 9RH
Tel: 020 7607 3637 / Fax: 020 7607 3629
e-mail: oberon.books@btinternet.com
www.oberonbooks.com

A *Gézagyerek* copyright © János Háy 2004

Translation copyright © Phil Porter 2004

János Háy is hereby identified as author of this play in
accordance with section 77 of the Copyright, Designs and
Patents Act 1988. The author has asserted his moral rights.

Phil Porter is hereby identified as author of this translation in
accordance with section 77 of the Copyright, Designs and
Patents Act 1988. The author has asserted his moral rights.

All rights whatsoever in this play are strictly reserved and
application for performance etc. should be made before
commencement of rehearsal to János Háy, hayjanos@freemail.hu.
No performance may be given unless a licence has been obtained,
and no alterations may be made in the title or the text of the play
without the author's prior written consent.

All rights whatsoever in this translation are strictly reserved and
application for performance etc. should be made before
commencement of rehearsal to The Peters, Fraser & Dunlop
Group Ltd, 34–43 Great Russell Street, London WC2B 5HA.
No performance may be given unless a licence has been
obtained, and no alterations may be made in the title or the text
of the play without the author's prior written consent.

This book is sold subject to the condition that it shall not by way
of trade or otherwise be circulated without the publisher's
consent in any form of binding or cover or circulated
electronically other than that in which it is published and
without a similar condition including this condition being
imposed on any subsequent purchaser.

A catalogue record for this book is available from the British
Library.

ISBN: 1 84002 467 4

Characters

GÉZA, a man, around 25, has learning difficulties,
shows some signs of autism

AUNTY RÓZSIKA, Géza's mother

LAJOS BANDA, a man, around 40,
works in the quarry, roughened by life

PITYU HERDA, a man, around 40,
works in the quarry, roughened by life

BÉLA KREKÁCS, around 40, pub man

LACI, a man, around 40, the boss at the quarry

NEIGHBOUR MAN, a neighbour,
same generation as Aunty Rózsika

NEIGHBOUR WOMAN, his wife

MARIKA, a woman, around 25, grocery shop assistant

VIZIKE, decrepit pub woman

KARESZ, a man, around 40, bus driver,
not so rough-looking as the other men

PUB PEOPLE

QUARRY PEOPLE

PRONUNCIATION GUIDE

Please note that in Hungarian pronunciation the stress is always on the first syllable.

Balog	[bologh]
Bárdi	[baardy]
Béla Krekács	[belah krekach]
Czeher	[tzeyer]
Dózsa	[dozjha]
Géza	[geezah]
Gyuri	[dew-ree]
Ilonka	[eehlonkah]
Imre	[eemreh]
Jani	[yoni]
Josó Tóth	[yoshow taught]
Karesz	[kores]
Kóbi	[korbi]
Kovács	[kovach]
Laci	[lotzi]
Lajos Banda	[loyosh bonda]
Marika	[morykah]
pálinka	[pa-len-kah]
Pityu Herda	[pityou]
Rák	[raakh]
Rózsika	[rou-zjhee-kah]
Sanyi	[shonyeh]
Szabó	[soboh]
Szob	[sob]
Vác	[vatz]
Vajsz	[voys]
Vilmos	[vhil-mosh]
Vizike	[vhi-zhi-keh]

ONE : ONE

Dawn. The bus stop on the main square of the village. There is also a grocery shop on the square. BANDA and HERDA are waiting at the stop.

BANDA: Fucking bus is late again. Drink?

BANDA offers HERDA a small bottle of spirit. He takes a swig.

HERDA: Again. It's downhill, it just needs to give itself a shove and roll down.

BANDA: If it don't start downhill means fucking nothing. The other day, Karesz heated the battery with a blowtorch, just to get it started.

HERDA: One day Karesz will blow himself up, then he'll be finished.

BANDA: This is it. (*BANDA drinks.*)

HERDA: He'll explode along with that bloody bus, and that'll be that.

BANDA drinks and gives the bottle back to HERDA.

BANDA: This morning, I woke up, such a massive burp and so bitter it was, I nearly spewed. And then when I spat the spit was pure yellow like snot.

HERDA: Spleen. I know this, it's the spleen.

BANDA: Long as it's not my liver.

HERDA: No, spleen not liver, I know this, liver turns your face like runny shit.

BANDA: Shat myself I did, I thought it was the liver, thought I'd spit my whole liver out, like I'm walking to

13

the bus and I'm spitting, and by the time I'm there I've got no liver left.

HERDA: It's the spleen, don't cack yourself. Spleen from all the pálinka brandy.

BANDA: But I didn't drink yesterday.

HERDA: How come?

BANDA: Just didn't.

HERDA: Maybe you forgot.

BANDA: Maybe I did.

BANDA drinks.

Maybe I did. Nothing went on yesterday anyhows.

HERDA: I don't know what you expected.

BANDA: Nothing.

RÓZSIKA arrives on her bike.

BOTH: (*Shouting.*) Aunty Rózsika! Aunty Rózsika…!

RÓZSIKA: Big baby, shouting out and scaring me, God's sake, I nearly fell off!

HERDA: Couldn't you see us standing here?

RÓZSIKA: Like hell am I looking out for you.

HERDA: Then why you twisting your neck round like an ostrich?

RÓZSIKA: I'm looking out for the bus, boy, the bus, and for Josó Tóth's son in that great jumbo of a tractor.

BANDA: But it's not coming, you can see that, the tractor makes a noise like a tank, you'd hear it, Aunty Rózsika, you'd hear it for definite.

RÓZSIKA: Fine, but I couldn't hear it the other day.

BANDA: Really?

RÓZSIKA: Because the wind blew against it, see, against the sound of the tractor.

BANDA: Against it?

HERDA: Against the tractor?

RÓZSIKA: Yes, the wind was blowing up and the tractor was coming down.

BANDA: Shit, so the wind blew the sound back, like it was coming but it wasn't coming, like whispering.

RÓZSIKA: This is it, Joso's son's hair blown completely back on end!

HERDA: Back on end against itself?

RÓZSIKA: Yeah, with the wind.

BANDA: Shit, this is a dangerous thing.

RÓZSIKA: All of a sudden the tractor is there where I am.

HERDA: Right by your bike.

RÓZSIKA: And the big cow of a thing is on top of me, so I can hardly get up on the pavement it's so close.

HERDA: Shit.

BANDA: Anyhows, that kid is stupid, that kid is really stupid.

HERDA: Josó Tóth's son has always been totally stupid, totally, totally stupid.

RÓZSIKA: Then he shouldn't be trusted with a tractor!

BANDA: So what then, a machine gun?

RÓZSIKA: You too can be damn stupid.

BANDA: But I don't have a tractor, that's the big difference.

HERDA: But you can whirr like a tractor, can't you?

BANDA: But I'm not whirring.

HERDA: Or the wind is blowing it away.

BANDA: What?

HERDA: The whirr.

RÓZSIKA: I'll heft my bike up on the pavement as long as we talk, so Josó Tóth's son doesn't run me over.

BANDA: But if I was making the noise, I couldn't…

RÓZSIKA: Couldn't what, Lajos?

HERDA: Drive a tractor.

BANDA: Speak, stupid, I couldn't speak!

HERDA: That's the truth, you can either speak or be a tractor.

HERDA and BANDA guffaw.

BANDA: Or you are Josó Tóth's son.

RÓZSIKA: Yes, well, I must go, Géza will be expecting his breakfast sausage.

She sets off then brakes.

So what did you want?

BANDA: So…we didn't want anything.

RÓZSIKA: Then I'll go if there's nothing.

BANDA: No, there was something though, wasn't there, Pityu?

HERDA: Oh... Yeah... Laci is looking for you.

RÓZSIKA: Laci?

HERDA: Boss Laci, from over the quarry.

RÓZSIKA: So what does he want?

BANDA: Oh, we don't know that. Or do we...?

HERDA: He'll tell you that.

RÓZSIKA: If he wants something I'm sure he'll tell me, that's true.

RÓZSIKA rides away.

ONE : TWO

Inside the village grocery shop. Morning.

MARIKA: Good morning, Aunty Rózsika!

RÓZSIKA: So, what's different, Marika? A day no better than any other.

MARIKA: Tell me about it, I could hardly scrape myself out of bed.

RÓZSIKA: Did anything go on yesterday?

MARIKA: The club was really pumping, Aunty Rózsika, we were there till one.

RÓZSIKA: Pumping, Marika? What were you pumping?

MARIKA: It's a disco, Aunty Rózsika, the beats were phat, really pumping.

RÓZSIKA: Fat beets? You go to the nightclub to pump fat beetroots?

MARIKA: Ugh, Aunty Rózsika, you're playing with me!

RÓZSIKA: I'm not.

MARIKA: You know, you must have seen it all on Satellite TV, haven't you?

RÓZSIKA: Hell, we don't get that one, just Slovak 1 and 2 of the foreign ones.

MARIKA: Phat, pumping, all it means is good.

RÓZSIKA: But you don't take those ecstatic tablets?

MARIKA: No way, Aunty Rózsika, the techno gets us high.

RÓZSIKA: Good for you.

MARIKA: Anyhows, Laci was looking for you.

RÓZSIKA: What did he want, didn't he say why?

MARIKA: He said it'd be better off in person, that he'd visit, he asked where you live because he hasn't been to the far end of the village in ten years.

RÓZSIKA: I suppose it's right not to leave messages, he should tell me if he wants something, shouldn't he?

MARIKA: He should. So, shoot, Aunty Rózsika.

RÓZSIKA: Shoot what?

MARIKA: As in what can I get you?

RÓZSIKA: The usual, Marika. Small loaf, milk, half pound off the sausage.

MARIKA: Isn't Géza bored of the sausage?

RÓZSIKA: He likes it, Marika, it's what he likes, bread and butter with sausage.

MARIKA: Every time?

RÓZSIKA: Every time.

ONE : THREE

The street outside RÓZSIKA's house. Her neighbour shouts...

MAN: Rózsika! Rózsika!

RÓZSIKA: What is it, Jani, what happened?

MAN: Laci from over the quarry was here, he was looking for you.

RÓZSIKA: Did Laci not say what he wanted?

MAN: No, but I think he was going on to Ironmonger Gyuri's house.

RÓZSIKA: He'll stop by again if he wants something, won't he?

RÓZSIKA is opening the front door when an old car brakes by her side.

LACI: Aunty Rózsika, good to find you at last!

RÓZSIKA: What is it, Laci, what do you want so much?

LACI: Aunty Rózsika, I have big news.

RÓZSIKA: Spit it out then, Laci, tell me.

LACI: The Germans have sent down that security's needed in the quarry, that they'll punish if it doesn't get safe enough...

RÓZSIKA: Well, the Germans know all about things, they always know what to do, at war too, everything was already lost but they still marched on.

LACI: What?

RÓZSIKA: Just like if it was a parade, but the Russians, like a rabble.

LACI: Oh, yeah, the Russians of course, them, for definite.

RÓZSIKA: Of course, they were all stealing.

LACI: They did steal.

RÓZSIKA: Even from children.

LACI: God yes, from them too.

RÓZSIKA: Even stole barrels they did.

LACI: Barrels?

RÓZSIKA: Oh yes.

LACI: Well, I wouldn't have expected that.

RÓZSIKA: What is it with the German, anyhows?

LACI: (*Enthuses.*) Well, they know the laws, they don't want anybody dying there, because then they've got to pay out.

RÓZSIKA: Pay out? They won't want that, that's for definite.

LACI: They know how to save money...

RÓZSIKA: Well, easy for them, they have money to save, isn't that right?

LACI: Well, they said...

RÓZSIKA: What?

LACI: (*Careful.*) Well...

RÓZSIKA: Well, well what?

LACI: Well, inspection is needed at the conveyor belt, otherwise they pay for accidents, so we got a bus driver seat from the bus people, and we put that in the middle where most of the belt can be seen, it is such a good bus driver seat, made of leathery plastic stuff, brown, looks very good, but now a driver is needed too… Do you get it, Aunty Rózsika?

RÓZSIKA: Yes, I get it, it's a bus driver's seat.

LACI: But someone needs to sit in it, do you get it, Aunty Rózsika?

RÓZSIKA: Yes, someone needs to sit in the seat, I get it…

LACI: You don't get it, Aunty Rózsika, you don't get it, we thought maybe Géza, Gézakid, that he'd be just right for it, then he'd have a job then, regular work…

RÓZSIKA: Thought Géza, that Géza should be…? Géza, my Géza??

LACI: Of course, Aunty Rózsika, I mean it'd suit Géza just right because the Germans, they don't want to pay much, you know how tight the purse strings are.

RÓZSIKA: You mean Géza would be the one?!

LACI: For definite, Aunty Rózsika, for definite, just talk it through with him, he can come tomorrow. Lajos Banda and Pityu Herda, they'll wait for him at the bus stop.

RÓZSIKA: Lajos and Pityu at the bus stop?

LACI: For definite, Aunty Rózsika, for definite, he can go with them, they'll sort him out, take care of him, you understand…

RÓZSIKA: I understand, of course I understand, Laci…

She is worried but happy, even weeping a bit.

Oh…oh my…well, I'll call Géza quick…

She rushes into the house.

ONE : FOUR

Kitchen. GÉZA is sitting by the range, staring at the black and greyish white pattern of the cheap kitchen floor.

RÓZSIKA: Little one, little one!

GÉZA: Good morning, Mum, good day, where have you been, the shop, and bought again the sausage and bread and milk, we'll have breakfast, I have been up, I have put my trousers on, my shirt, you're not drinking coffee...

RÓZSIKA: Listen now, listen for just a moment.

GÉZA: I'm listening, Mum, I am, I'm just counting how many black stones and how many grey stones on the floor, but I always mess up, how many black and how many grey, I always mess up the counting.

RÓZSIKA: Leave that now, let it go, Laci was here just now.

GÉZA: What Laci, do I know Laci, do I know him?

RÓZSIKA: Laci from over the quarry, Boss Laci.

GÉZA: Laci works in the quarry, I know that, and Uncle Lajos Banda works there too, and Uncle Pityu Herda works there too, and the quarry is where Laci works, I know that.

RÓZSIKA: Well, you can go and work there from tomorrow, Laci said that. Do you get that, little one? Laci said that you can go too.

GÉZA: All right, so Laci said that, but what would I do in the quarry? I can't work there, you know that, I can't go there, I mustn't, Mum knows too that I mustn't. (*Catches his breath.*) Who'll watch the kitchen floor? Who'll watch over the house? Who? I can't be a worker because I can't do the tasks, you know that, I can't leave home because

I'll get in trouble, the doctor said that too, I mustn't do a job because I'll get in trouble...

RÓZSIKA: It's not a job like that, it's perfect for you. There's a chair like bus drivers have.

GÉZA: But what is the chair like? Where is the chair? I don't know.

RÓZSIKA: The chair is like, like that brown leathery plastic stuff, like on the buses, you know, one like that above the belt.

GÉZA: I get it, the chair is above the belt, I get it.

RÓZSIKA: And you sit there and mind the stones go properly along the belt.

GÉZA: But that's it. That's exactly what I'm scared of, that I don't know, that I don't know when they go properly, and what do I do if they don't go properly? I mustn't get excited, the lady doctor in Vác, she told me that I mustn't.

RÓZSIKA: But you can go to work like the rest, like Uncle Lajos Banda and Uncle Pityu Herda.

GÉZA: Like Uncle Lajos Banda, and Uncle Pityu Herda?

RÓZSIKA: And you'll get wages, and we'll get your father's bag, the shoulder bag, it's still in the attic.

GÉZA: Dad's bag?

RÓZSIKA: For definite Dad's bag. I'll put your food in it. Every morning I'll pack bread and butter and sausage for you, and a bottle of fizzy squash...

GÉZA: (*Staring, upper body rocking.*) Am I going along Dózsa Street with the bag on my shoulder, with the bag?

RÓZSIKA: Yes, just like when your father was alive, all along the street.

GÉZA: I'm going to the bus stop, with the bag on my shoulder at the bus stop.

RÓZSIKA: Right there, right there for the five-thirty bus.

GÉZA: And Uncle Lajos Banda and Uncle Pityu Herda will be there.

RÓZSIKA: For definite, they'll be expecting you.

GÉZA: Then we'll go to town, to the pit at Szob.

RÓZSIKA: You will, you'll be there all day, you'll work properly, and you'll come back in the evening, you'll go to the pub with Uncle Banda and his lot, then you'll come home for supper.

GÉZA: The money, when will I get it, the money?

RÓZSIKA: At the start of the month, I suppose, you get the money at the start of the month.

GÉZA: Will I go to work with Uncle Banda and Uncle Herda?

RÓZSIKA: For definite. Exactly that.

GÉZA: Will I go to work, will I watch the stones in the quarry on the belt? (*Stammers.*) Will I get to watch the stones in the quarry? Is this real? Is this real that I get to watch the stones at the quarry, is this real, will I be the stone watcher? Are they not going to call me Géza The Kid? Are they going to call me Stonewatcher? Are they going to say Géza is a stonewatcher at the quarry? Géza Stonewatcher, they'll say. Géza Stonewatcher and not that Gézakid?

RÓZSIKA: Not that.

ONE : FIVE

GÉZA speaks to his father's portrait.

GÉZA: I'm going down the street, Dad. Going down. And the dogs are barking. Uncle Lajos and Uncle Pityu already there. I'm telling them, here I am, Uncle Lajos, I'm coming to work as well. Just like Dad went to work, just the same, just like any other person, Dad. I'm not damaged, it's how I am. I'm not damaged. This isn't like an illness. Mum said that you, Dad, you expected this thing to pass like the measles, like with the red spots. So, one day, you, Dad, you could say the kid's not damaged no more. But I'm not damaged, Dad, I'm not, it's how I am. I'm going down the street just like uncle Lajos, to work. The dogs bark, so they should. Mum said Dad went on, like, the kid will outgrow it, he'd say stop doing this, kid, and stop doing that, kid, as well, but I couldn't stop doing it because that's the way I had to do it. And Dad used to tell Mum, don't let the kid make faces like he's mad, don't let him laugh that way or he'll stay like that forever. Said Dad to Mum. And Mum went then what should she do with me, that's what Mum went. And Dad went back like I'm this way because of Mum, is why I still haven't outgrown it. I'm not at school any more and still I haven't outgrown it. Dad said it's all Mum's fault, I should have got better long time ago if Mum wasn't letting me do everything. And Dad was shouting at Mum that it's going to stay like this forever. Then he didn't speak to any of us. He didn't tell me, come on, Géza, come to the quarry with me. He just went. Dad went to the quarry. To the quarry, every morning. I'm going now, Dad, going down to the bus, Dad. I'm not damaged, Dad. I would have gone to the quarry with Dad as well if you'd asked. I would have gone, because I'm not damaged, Dad. It's how I am. If I wasn't this way I wouldn't be Géza, I wouldn't, Dad. I wouldn't be to

Mum what I am now, I wouldn't. I'd be someone else, not Géza, Dad. I'd be someone…

ONE : SIX

Next morning in the street. GÉZA is walking to the bus stop. Dogs are barking.

GÉZA: So what you barking for, what you barking for in the yard? Woof, woof, woof, woof, woof, woof. (*Bangs bag against fence.*) Barking all day long, woof, woof, woof, all day long.

HERDA: Come on, Géza, bus will be here any minute, come on!

GÉZA: Woof, woof, woof, all day long, woof, woof, woof. (*Banging his bag against the fence.*)

BANDA: Leave them dogs alone now, Gézakid!

GÉZA: Good morning, good work, good day.

BANDA / HERDA: Hello Géza, hi.

GÉZA: Uncle Lajos, what did Aunty Ilonka put in for you, what did she put in?

BANDA: Bread and lard, pálinka brandy she didn't pack, but I bought me a quarter bottle in the grocery, didn't I, Pityu?

BANDA takes a swig and HERDA does the same.

Well, what have you got?

GÉZA: Bread and butter with sausage, Uncle Lajos, I have bread and butter with sausage and fizzy raspberry squash…

HERDA: Fizzy squash, well, it's a very dangerous drink, son, very dangerous. Drives the lime from your bones, you're not even grown old but you've no bones left in your body any more, and then you collapse like a stinking piece of rag. Like a heap of diarrhoea, not so much a shitty man as a man made out of shit.

GÉZA: (*Staring, eyes wide.*) Collapse, you collapse...?

BANDA: You're stupid, Pityu, completely stupid, pumping all shades of shit into the kid's head. Anyhows, don't lean into my face, your breath stinks like a propane-butane cylinder just exploded in your stomach.

BANDA and HERDA laugh.

HERDA: You know what, that's the smell of your face bouncing back off mine, reverberating, like an echo. (*They laugh.*)

GÉZA: (*Squeezing his fingers and hands.*) I have all my bones, I have them all, and I've even got two in my arm, just down here, so if the fizzy water washes one away, I'll still have one left. Uncle Pityu, I'll still have one more left. (*Proud of his idea.*)

BANDA: Pityu's stupid, Géza, he's Stupidman, his head's like a bog into which the world has taken a shit...

The bus arrives. Doors open.

What happened, Karesz? Did your whanger get stuck in your woman?

KARESZ: Leave me alone with your rubbish, Lajos.

HERDA: That's not it, he lost it while he was having a piss.

KARESZ: It's been shitty enough already, all right, the battery died, I had to wake up Jani Balog and get his out of his, that's why I'm behind, but if you quit shitting about then I'll catch up by Szob and the schoolkids won't miss their train.

HERDA: Good, because Laci bollocked me badly the other day for being late, says it'll be him the German sacks if we don't start work on time.

BANDA: Anyhows, isn't it time they bought a couple of new buses, one day it'll fall apart on a bend, they'll be scraping up all the bits with teaspoons to put the passengers back together…

KARESZ: German didn't buy us up, did he, how the fuck do we buy a new bus? On the money you pay us?

HERDA: Yeah, on the money we pay you.

KARESZ: Look, it's only cheap fares left on this route, half schoolkids, the other half pensioners, they ride for nothing…

BANDA: All right, Karesz, cut blathering on, let's go.

KARESZ: Anyhows, you still work on that old belt.

BANDA: It's perfectly good, isn't it, Pityu?

HERDA: For definite, just like brand new.

KARESZ: You're talking rubbish, Pityu, absolute shit. When did the quarry buy that, must be twenty-five years ago. For all the cash the German's got he don't give a shit about new machinery, you see, don't give a shit.

HERDA: However, however.

KARESZ: What do you mean, however?

HERDA: Géza has been brought in to work as a stonewatcher, owing to safety precautions…

KARESZ: You are pulling my pisser, Gézakid?!

BANDA: Gézakid, as a stonewatcher.

GÉZA: Good morning, Mister Karesz, good day, good work. (*Pushes his way into view.*)

KARESZ: Hello Géza, you're not joining the slog, are you?

GÉZA: I'm going to work, Mister Karesz, I've got my bread and butter in my bag.

KARESZ: (*Astonished.*) Really?!

GÉZA: I need a ticket, Mister Karesz, I don't have my pass yet, so I need a ticket now, Mister Karesz, a ticket, that's what I want…

KARESZ: Come on, Géza, I'll take you for free, least I can do, isn't it, I'm driving the bus anyhows, ain't I?!

GÉZA: I've got money for the ticket, I have money thank you, Mister Karesz.

BANDA: Come on, Géza, move inside and shut up, you hear?! (*Pushes him in.*)

HERDA: Look at that, Géza! You'll have a seat just like this. (*Points at seat.*)

GÉZA: I'll have a seat just like this too, I'll be the driver, I'll have a seat like this. I know, Uncle Laci told Mum, he said I'd have a seat like that.

KARESZ: But there'll be no wheel.

GÉZA: No, only the seat.

KARESZ: No accelerator either.

GÉZA: No, not that either.

HERDA: It's not a bus, Karesz, not a bus it's a quarry.

KARESZ: Okay, I'm having a conversation with Géza.

HERDA: (*Genuine.*) Oh, that's different, if it's a conversation that's totally different.

ONE : SEVEN

In the quarry before work starts. There is a conveyor belt and a shack, on the side are live workings, high up in the middle is the seat.

BANDA: Boss, it's Gézakid, we brought him along.

LACI: *(Patting GÉZA on back.)* Hi Géza, glad you came.

GÉZA: Good morning, Uncle Laci, good morning.
Everything went very well, I came on the bus with Uncle Pityu Herda and Uncle Lajos Banda...

LACI: Can you see that chair high above the assembly?

GÉZA: I can see that, Uncle Laci, of course I can see that.

LACI: Well, that is going to be your throne.

GÉZA: That? I see.

BANDA: You'll be like a king... You see...

HERDA: Absolutely, like a king up there.

LACI: Come on, I'll show you what to do.

They go up to the chair. BANDA and HERDA shout up...

BANDA: Listen, Géza, listen hard.

HERDA: This is the thing Géza, yeah, it's why you're here.

GÉZA: I'll learn, Uncle Lajos, I'll learn.

LACI: Well, these here are the controls, see that?

GÉZA: I see that, Uncle Laci, the controls.

LACI: You sit here and you watch the belt.

GÉZA: I watch the belt.

LACI: If you see something suspicious then you press the red, see, it stops.

GÉZA: I see, I see, I'm pressing the red, it stops, it stops on red.

LACI: You can start it up with green, you see, you'll start up when they give the sign.

GÉZA: I see, I'm pressing red, it stops, I'm pressing green, it starts, it goes, it starts when I press, like remote control telly, off on red.

LACI: Press it, have a practice.

GÉZA presses the button, the belt stops. He laughs. He plays with it and the belt starts and stops and starts etc.

GÉZA: Red, off...green, on...red, off...green, on...off...on...off...on...off...on...

LACI: Good enough.

LACI grabs the controls, stops the belt and gives them back.

From now on you only press if something happens, see? If a big stone crashes on the belt, or if the stone gets mixed up with earth, and most importantly when there's an accident, you see, if someone falls on the belt, you see?

GÉZA: (*Nods.*) I see, if something happens, I see, a big stone, if I see a big stone, that's when, and if there's an accident.

BANDA: See, Géza, no problem, just like pissing, when you need to, you just pull out your plonker.

GÉZA: I see, I see, this is it, off is red, on is green, I see, I watch, watch all day, from my chair, like a king, Uncle Laci said that, all day long like a king.

The belt starts up and work kicks off.

ONE : EIGHT

In the street. NEIGHBOUR MAN and NEIGHBOUR WOMAN stand by their fence. RÓZSIKA approaches on her bike.

WOMAN: She's coming back from the shop already, look.

MAN: Who is?

WOMAN: Rózsika.

RÓZSIKA: (*Stops by the fence.*) Morning.

WOMAN: Morning, Rózsika, you're coming from the shop already.

RÓZSIKA: Oh yes, got to do the shopping every day now.

WOMAN: Every day? Why've you got to do it every day?

RÓZSIKA: Because I've got to pack food for Géza.

WOMAN: Really? Why've you got to pack food for him?

RÓZSIKA: Because he goes to work over the quarry in Szob…

MAN: So that's why we saw the kid this morning. We saw him walking down the street…

WOMAN: Only we didn't know what he was doing, or why so early, or where to. Banging his bag on the fence he was, the dogs were really howling.

MAN: It's their job, isn't it?

RÓZSIKA: Anyhows, that's where he goes, to the quarry.

WOMAN: So that's why Laci from the quarry was after you yesterday.

RÓZSIKA: That's right, it's why he kept on leaving me messages.

WOMAN: Suddenly it all makes sense.

RÓZSIKA: I know the kid's faulty, but even he's good for something, now he's got a kind of job anyhows…

MAN: What did Laci find for Géza, what did he find?

RÓZSIKA: He watches if the stones go all right along the belt.

WOMAN: Really?

MAN: Why do you got to watch that, what for?

RÓZSIKA: Because the German doesn't want to pay for accidents.

MAN: I see, so the German wanted it, I thought Laci had the idea just so Géza had something.

RÓZSIKA: Laci said if there was no surveillance then the insurance wouldn't pay if there was an accident, wouldn't pay, but the German would have to pay the damages.

WOMAN: In other words, it's because of the paying.

RÓZSIKA: This is it, the kid's over there now, watching the belt there…

WOMAN: That is perfect for Géza.

MAN: Perfect for him, he's found his place, that Géza. (*Laughs.*)

RÓZSIKA: Now he's getting used for something after all, isn't he?

MAN: That's right, now he's doing something after all.

RÓZSIKA: If he only sits in the kitchen, he gets nowhere.

WOMAN: Nowhere, that's for definite.

RÓZSIKA: As for me, what do I know how long I'll be around, then what'll happen to him?

MAN: One must think about that as well, this is it.

WOMAN: It's perfect like this, Rózsika, the kid's got a place after all.

RÓZSIKA: I could see on him, when I was packing his lunch, how proud he was, looking at his father's picture on the dresser, and he was mumbling to himself, I could feel a little teardrop running up to my eyes, him standing there at the dresser looking at his father's picture, and he was mumbling something, I backed up to the kitchen so he could still stand there, because I didn't want to be the one to hush him away and stop him standing at the dresser as long as he pleases, but then he came through, and his eyes were shining…electricity gleaming in his eyes so…

MAN: It'll definitely be good for him there.

WOMAN: That's for definite, it's for him, that's for definite.

RÓZSIKA: I know how hard it is to understand if you've not got such a faulty child, I know that…

MAN: Well, one has a faulty one, the other doesn't, this is how it is.

RÓZSIKA: But people don't know what it's like.

WOMAN: We know, Rózsika, we saw how hard you worked for this child.

RÓZSIKA: It doesn't matter how he's like, he's mine after all, isn't he?

MAN: This is it.

RÓZSIKA: He's my blood after all, and that of his father's.

WOMAN: This is it, Rózsika, we understand.

RÓZSIKA: Well, got to go now. It's good that I can talk at least to you a bit, I can tell you at least, and after all you're fond of Géza, after all…

MAN: Géza's a good kid, good kid, Rózsika, that's for definite, that kid's a good one.

RÓZSIKA: Well, I'm really going now.

They say goodbye. RÓZSIKA goes, MAN and WOMAN stay.

WOMAN: I don't know...

MAN: What?

WOMAN: What that foolchild can do at the quarry, what on earth...?

MAN: He doesn't do anything but sits, and stares straight ahead, like at home too, he watches the stones, that's what he does...

WOMAN: I just don't believe he couldn't have been sent to a school where they would have taught him something, after all, they say they teach even the blind how to work, and read, and everything, I just don't believe he couldn't have been enrolled for something like that... Even the blind...

MAN: She was worried about the kid, she must have been worried about the kid, like what's going to happen with her not around, all on his own, yeah, some school, far away, what he'd do on his own...

WOMAN: She was worried about the money, that's what, she didn't want to spend on him... The money, that's what she was bothered about. Instead she kept him here so he remains stupid...

MAN: Stupid he remained, that's for definite, that's for definite, he remained completely stupid...

WOMAN: He's got a job anyhows, he did that anyhows.

MAN: If he did, so what if he did?

WOMAN: And they sent you away.

MAN: The quarry was up shit creek, that's why, because it was up the shit.

WOMAN: But they didn't want you back when the German bought it. They didn't want you back, just Banda and Herda.

MAN: (*Restrains himself.*) No, Banda and Herda are both younger than me, that's why.

WOMAN: And now he wants Géza, he even wants him too.

MAN: (*Yelling.*) Enough, leave it!

WOMAN: What you yelling now for, what do you have yell for, what is it, does the truth hurt, that's what's hurting you...

MAN: Shut up, stop it, stop going on, all right, stop going on because I'm going to beat you up, all right, I'm going to beat you up.

WOMAN: Nothing's going to change from you yelling, no good in that.

MAN: Only that I'm going to beat you up, that's the good. It's enough for me that I beat you up.

WOMAN: You wouldn't dare to do even that. Because you're such a nobody, you'd only get noticed in comparison to Géza, compared with the retard boy, otherwise you're nothing, you get that, you've achieved nothing in your whole life, nothing, at least you were someone compared to Géza at least, but now you're not even that...

MAN: Because I married you, that's why, because I married you, that's why I'm like this, because you're the one I married, that's why.

They fight. A scuffle.

ONE : NINE

Noon at the quarry.

BANDA: Look at the kid, the way he's sitting there.

HERDA: Like a god, that's what he's like in the chair.

BANDA: The kid's happy now, very happy.

LACI: (*Shouts.*) We're stopping, lunch time, we're stopping!

The belt stops. GÉZA remains in his seat.

BANDA: Come on, Géza, we're eating!

HERDA: Yeah, come on!

GÉZA works himself out of his seat and they all sit down by the belt.

GÉZA: Nothing went on but I kept watching, Uncle Lajos.

BANDA: The important thing is you were watching.

GÉZA: Good lard, Uncle Lajos, is it good?

BANDA: It's good. What you eating?

GÉZA: Bread and butter, Uncle Lajos, bread and butter and fizzy squash.

HERDA: Harmful stuff, the fizzy squash.

BANDA: Leave the kid alone, Pityu.

Pause. They are eating.

HERDA: We'll get through the afternoon, then we'll go to the pub.

BANDA: That's for definite.

GÉZA: I'll go to the pub as well, I will as well.

BANDA: Really, are you coming too?

GÉZA: Mum said I'll go to the pub too, and go home only after that.

HERDA: Absolutely he's coming along, absolutely.

BANDA: Did you hear Vilmos hanged himself?

HERDA: Bloody hell! Is he dead?

BANDA: He's in hospital.

HERDA: Did he go mental or what?

BANDA: Apparently, his old woman hid the cellar keys, and he wanted a drink, goes for the wine, from the cellar, only the key's not there, no key.

HERDA: So he hanged himself, that Vilmos is stupid, completely stupid. Instead of slapping the old woman round the phizog.

GÉZA: Stupid Vilmos, completely stupid.

BANDA: That's what he should have done, that's what, plug her in the face, that woman.

HERDA: He's so stupid, God Almighty, he's so stupid. Round ours, this would never happen. We don't even have a cellar.

BANDA: Yes, this is a big difference.

HERDA: This is, yes, big, but anyhows, even if we had one, not even then, see.

BANDA: I see, but you've not got a cellar anyhows, have you?

HERDA: No, but I'm saying if I had one.

BANDA: If you had one, but how do I know what would happen, when you haven't, see?

HERDA: One would imagine if there was one, not even then, I don't believe it would happen.

BANDA: But I can't imagine that there is one because there isn't one, and if there isn't one there isn't one.

HERDA: (*Pensive.*) All right, let's leave it.

GÉZA: (*Has followed their conversation.*) It's half past noon, Uncle Lajos, Uncle Pityu, Uncle Laci will start the belt, he'll start it soon.

BANDA: All right, kid, all right.

LACI: We're going!

The belt starts to move.

GÉZA: I said it was half past noon, didn't I? I know it, I told you.

BANDA: You're like a clock.

HERDA: That's for definite, you can set your radio to Géza, that's for definite.

BANDA: How come the radio? I don't get it.

HERDA: The news.

BANDA: Oh, the news. (*Pause.*) But why?

HERDA: I don't know, just...

BANDA: Yeah, that's true.

HERDA: What?

BANDA: The radio.

ONE : TEN

*Early evening in the pub. BANDA, HERDA, GÉZA, KREKÁCS
and VIZIKE are there.*

GÉZA: Did I do well, Uncle Lajos? I did well, did I do well,
didn't I?

BANDA: Just like you should, Géza, just right... Just like
you should...

HERDA: Géza's become a decent man now.

KREKÁCS: How come decent?

HERDA: Like the rest of us.

KREKÁCS: He has?

HERDA: He has. He goes to work in the morning.

GÉZA: I go to work, I'm going in the morning, I'm going
to work in the morning.

KREKÁCS: Night shift... (*Lewd gesture.*) You doing that
too?

GÉZA: In the morning I go, in the morning.

HERDA: Leave the kid alone. You loaf round all day at
home.

KREKÁCS: How much more do you get compared to the
dole, eh, how much?

BANDA: You get paid out of my work.

KREKÁCS: Out of that, fuck, I couldn't even pay the child
care out of that.

HERDA: How do you think you're getting dole? Where
from, in your opinion?

KREKÁCS: The council pays it, yeah, the mayor pays it upfront.

BANDA: Anyhows, so stupid you are, you'd never get hired anyhows, you couldn't even watch stones. With your baggy eyes.

HERDA: By ten in the morning your eyes are glazed over, you suck yourself full of booze that early.

KREKÁCS: Why, what are you like, what the fuck are you like? So tell us, what happened last night, what happened then?

BANDA: Why, what happened then?

HERDA: Nothing happened, not one thing, for definite.

KREKÁCS: If you don't remember nothing, well, must mean nothing happened.

HERDA: Why, were you even in the pub?

KREKÁCS: You didn't ask first, I did, that's the order of it. When he's told us what happened then you ask the questions, all right?

BANDA: Problem is, fuck you, you've got all day to think, you can think on the dole, but we're working, and Géza too, at the quarry.

KREKÁCS: At the quarry, didn't say you don't, but now we could really tell Géza what the tools are meant for.

BANDA: What tools?

HERDA: The shovel or what?

KREKÁCS: In addition to the having of a piss, yeah?

HERDA: In addition to the having of a piss, one also uses the shovel, or what?

KREKÁCS: Pityu, when did you last see your wife, I'm serious, your brain is slowing down.

HERDA: I saw her yesterday.

KREKÁCS: And do you remember this or just believe it to be the case?

HERDA: Well, you don't remember things that are always the same.

BANDA: I reckon you just heard her.

HERDA: How come just heard her?

BANDA: Well, her snoring, that's what you heard. Not because it was so dark, not because of that, just because you couldn't see anything any more, blind drunk, not even the darkness.

HERDA: But what about the tools?

GÉZA: So I get to know what they're for, but I do know.

HERDA: See, Géza knows.

KREKÁCS: Well, Géza knows but you sure don't.

HERDA: Don't know what?

KREKÁCS: Well, what do you think, what the fuck, exactly that, exactly the fuck, do you think the tool is good for?

BANDA guffaws.

HERDA: Oh, is that what you mean?

KREKÁCS: This is it, finally you get it. Well, we could pay Vizike to screw Géza. We'll club together, yeah, free screw, yeah, club together no problem.

BANDA: See, that is just what Géza needs.

GÉZA: (*Gets frightened.*) I mustn't, I'm not allowed.

KREKÁCS: You must, Géza, you are allowed.

GÉZA: The lady doctor told me in the city, she said in the city that I mustn't yet.

BANDA: Know what she told me, that doctor in the city, do you know what she said, said I shouldn't drink brandy or wine or I'd die, she said…

GÉZA: (*Nervous.*) She said that, she said that…?

BANDA: And know when she said that, do you know when?

GÉZA: When did she say that, when?

BANDA: Five years ago, five years and still nothing wrong.

KREKÁCS: Géza, has your dick fallen off or what, go for it, yeah, go for it, Géza…

GÉZA: She told me at the hospital, she told me I mustn't…

HERDA: They're not worth shit, doctors, they just rake in the backhanders. Uncle Jani Szabó says he slipped his doctor ten thousand forints when half his stomach got taken out.

BANDA: Ten thousand, that's something, ten thousand.

HERDA: But you know what he was told?

KREKÁCS: What?

HERDA: Doctor told him it wasn't enough, yeah, ten thousand not enough!

BANDA: Bloody hell!

HERDA: So Uncle Jani said his stomach wasn't enough either because half of it had been taken out! (*They all guffaw.*) Not enough, yeah, that pillock in Vác said not enough…

BANDA: Where do they get the cheek, where do they get the bollocks, just hold out their hand and pocket the money in a blink. In a blink for all you earn in half a year. One blink!

HERDA: But the local doctor is something too, visits with his compulsory vaccinations, Uncle Lajos Kóbi says the local doctor does his visits, yeah, with that free medicine stuff that's free for old people, then he says he had to import it from abroad, yeah, and it's so expensive and it cost him too, and takes two thousand forints each off the old ladies, and where there's two people, if the husband's still alive, then it's four thousand, yeah, four thousand...

KREKÁCS: Better off with one of them dead, then you get away cheaper, don't you?

GÉZA: We didn't pay in the city, we didn't pay, Mum didn't pay because she didn't want us to, the lady doctor said Aunty Rózsika shouldn't pay because it was free, free.

BANDA: You were very lucky, very lucky because some doctors you'd lose the shirt off your back.

GÉZA: But I can pay now because I earn money, I'm an earner, I'll get money at the start of the month like anyone.

KREKÁCS: Know what, Géza, that money you should give to Vizike, better use of it, even Vizike is a better use of it...

GÉZA: But I can't, Uncle Béla, I can't.

BANDA: You could try, Géza, least have a go, you thought the same about the quarry, like you couldn't, you thought just the same about that, didn't you?

GÉZA: But not this, Uncle Lajos, I can't. Well, I'm going now, goodbye, I'm going home, it's seven o'clock, I'll see you tomorrow, goodbye, bye bye, see you tomorrow!

HERDA: Bye, Géza, bye, don't be late in the morning, bus don't wait.

GÉZA: I know, Uncle Pityu, I won't be late, I won't be late in the morning.

GÉZA leaves the pub.

KREKÁCS: In your opinion, if somebody is like that up there (*points at his head*) is he not working down there too?

BANDA: No way, like anyone else, they've got children too, even the blind have got them, I already saw at the hospital.

HERDA: Saw what, retards with kids?

BANDA: This is it, yeah, this is it, and they were sneaking out to the bushes, like big-headed men, and big-headed women, made me puke.

KREKÁCS: You puked, why did you puke?

BANDA: It was like, I had a good look, it was like, I just had to puke, seeing what was going on in the bush, it was like that.

HERDA: Naked, like anyone else?

BANDA: Like anyone else, even taking it in the mouth, yeah, in the mouth. And I'm behind the window looking on and puking, puked all over the lino.

KREKÁCS: Shit, I wouldn't have thought that.

HERDA: What, that Lajos would puke?

KREKÁCS: No, that they do this, that's what.

BANDA: They sure do.

KREKÁCS: And their children will be stupid too or what?

HERDA: The blind have kids that see, makes no difference they're blind.

KREKÁCS: Then Géza could have normal kids.

HERDA: For definite.

KREKÁCS: I wouldn't have thought that, for definite I wouldn't have. So, is it possible I'm more clever than my dad?

BANDA: It is possible because your dad was extremely stupid.

HERDA: To be more stupid than him is in itself a form of art.

KREKÁCS: I wouldn't have thought that, I really wouldn't.

ONE : ELEVEN

Late evening at home, in the kitchen.

RÓZSIKA: You tired out, little one?

GÉZA: I was watching close, Mum, I was watching close, the stone… Like this. (*Imitates watching the stone.*) I was watching the stone like this, each lump of stone, they quarry the grey stones there, light grey stone on the belt, I was watching that, watching it close so nothing happens, watching hard I was.

RÓZSIKA: But nothing went on, nothing I hope?!

GÉZA: Nothing went on, Mum, because I was watching, and if something did go on, I just press the red button, if something did go on, but nothing went on.

RÓZSIKA: Was Uncle Lajos there?

GÉZA: He was, Mum.

RÓZSIKA: And was Uncle Pityu there too?

GÉZA: He was, Mum.

RÓZSIKA: Did you eat your bread?

GÉZA: I did, Mum. And Uncle Lajos brought lard.

RÓZSIKA: Lard?

GÉZA: That's what he brought.

RÓZSIKA: Here's your dinner.

RÓZSIKA puts a plate of food in front of GÉZA.

GÉZA: (*Eating.*) Thanks, Mum, thanks for the dinner.

RÓZSIKA: Eat up, little one, you must have a bigger appetite after all that hard work, you must be hungry...

GÉZA: It's better now, Mum, tastes better now because I was watching close. Even Uncle Lajos said I was watching fine, just fine...

ONE : TWELVE

It is morning and GÉZA is walking down the street waving his bag. Dogs are barking.

GÉZA: What you barking for again, what you barking for, huh, woof-woof? All day long barking here, woof-woof, just barking, you're so stupid, so much stupid, woof-woof.

MAN: You off again, Géza?

GÉZA: Every day, Uncle Jani, I'm going to go every day now.

MAN: Is it good there, kid, do you like it?

GÉZA: I watch the stones, on the belt, I'm watching so there's no trouble, Uncle Jani, I watch all day, I know how to. I've got a red button, I've got that, and I've got a green one too, Uncle Jani.

MAN: So you've got the buttons eh, kid?

GÉZA: I do, Uncle Jani, I switch off when needed, switch off if there's trouble, off.

BANDA: Run, Géza, trudging along like a blind mouse, the bus is coming...

GÉZA: I'm coming, I am, I'm just having a chat with Uncle Jani.

BANDA: Shit, we were about to think you wouldn't make it on time.

GÉZA: I'm on time, Uncle Lajos, bang on time, Mister Karesz is late, is Mister Karesz late again?

HERDA: He is, because the bus is shit, that's why he's late.

GÉZA: What's in your bag there, Uncle Lajos, anyhows?

BANDA: What the shit do you think, lard, bread, quarter-bottle from the shop, you?

GÉZA: Bread, butter and sausage and a bottle of fizzy squash, Uncle Lajos.

HERDA: That's good, but just watch it doesn't wash the lime out of you...

BANDA: I thought that once you'd said it you'd forget about that lime thing.

HERDA: I don't forget it because that's how it is.

BANDA: I hate it when you talk right in my face, I hate it, it's like being sprayed with some insecticide sprinkler, you gobbing all over my face, gobbing saliva. One day, I'll end up with all the skin rotted off from my cheeks.

GÉZA: Uncle Lajos, I can hear Mister Karesz coming, I can hear the bus coming.

The bus rolls up, the doors open.

BANDA: What the fuck this time, Karesz, you switched the battery yesterday.

KARESZ: Yeah, but I had to give it back to Jani Balog last night so he could use it, then this morning I had to ask for it again, thought I'd shit my pants lugging it, completely full of lead it is, solid lead.

GÉZA: Good morning, Mister Karesz, we'll catch up by Szob so the school-kids don't miss their connection, Uncle Karesz, so they don't miss it.

KARESZ: All right, kid, have you got your pass now?

GÉZA: Naturally, Mister Karesz, naturally, I got it from Uncle Laci yesterday so I can go every day now, so I can go.

KARESZ: All right, I'm closing the doors, mind your back, Pityu!

The doors close, the engine roars and the bus leaves. RÓZSIKA arrives at the neighbours' fence on her bike.

MAN: The kid's gone, Rózsika.

RÓZSIKA: Yes, gone for the day.

The dogs bark.

What do those beasts howl for every time I come past?

WOMAN: Your mudguard's crackling, Rózsika, that's why, the mudguard makes that crackling noise.

RÓZSIKA: They should know by now my mudguard crackles, it always has, hasn't it?

MAN: They're meant to bark, that's what they're in charge of.

RÓZSIKA: That's right, that's for definite.

WOMAN: Anyhows, how much does Géza earn?

RÓZSIKA: We don't know yet but the German needs him for the insurance, so he gets something.

WOMAN: But how much can it be?

RÓZSIKA: I don't know, I really don't know.

RÓZSIKA rides away on her bike.

MAN: He can't get much, not for that job.

WOMAN: But he gets something, for definite, he gets something.

MAN: That's what I'm saying, he earns, but not that much.

WOMAN: Point is he earns, he's got a job for which he earns something.

MAN: Now, why do you keep on saying the same thing, what you getting at, he earns and that's that, good for him.

WOMAN: That's what I'm getting at, exactly that.

MAN: How hard did I try to get hired, how hard, what are you twisting the knife for, why are you twisting the knife, because I made the effort but if you're over fifty you're not needed, all right, not needed over fifty, not even the German wants you over fifty, not needed.

WOMAN: He just needs that little spastic, him he needs.

ONE : THIRTEEN

In the morning, by the conveyor belt.

LACI: I don't care when you come in but the German will rip your bollocks off if he finds out we start fifteen minutes late every day, all right, he'll add the whole lot up, his brain's like a calculator without the clicking noises.

BANDA: All right, Laci, we can't help it, that fucking bus, you see!

LACI: I see but the German won't, German don't give a shit about the bus, German needs eight hours of work done, more if possible.

HERDA: Why the fuck exactly did you have to sell it to the German, why the fuck?

LACI: Because, fuck's sake, only he had the money, see, only him. If he ditches it then it's washed up, kaput, that's it.

BANDA: All right, Laci, I get it, but basically, it's just nothing to this German, this quarry, it's nothing, he doesn't know the first motorway was built out of here, he doesn't know that.

HERDA: And Metro Line Two.

GÉZA: Metro Line Two?

HERDA: For definite, Metro Line Two.

GÉZA: That too?

HERDA: For definite, Metro Line Two too.

BANDA: I mean, the German don't care about it either, see, he don't care, it just can't be right, fuck's sake, that the country was built from this stone and now the quarry's not good for anything, and nobody from home wants it, I don't get how it pays better for the German than us, all right, I just don't get it.

HERDA: This is very true, how Lajos puts it.

LACI: Nobody wanted it.

BANDA: Well, this is it, but why nobody wanted it, that's what I don't get.

LACI: Because no-one had the cash, just him, and as for why it works for him, and how it pays off for him, I don't know, but it pays off for definite, you see, there's a lot of new roads being built, see...

HERDA: All right, fuck the German for a game of stone soldiers, let's get going!

BANDA: All right, let's go, get in place, Géza, we're going to start it...

GÉZA: (*Climbs to his seat.*) Start, attention, I'm paying attention, start Uncle Laci, let's go. (*Gives his commands like a Sergeant Major.*)

HERDA: Like a god, Géza, sitting up there.

BANDA: Yeah, total god, like in a painting, peeping through the clouds.

HERDA: You wouldn't have thought it a week ago, not this, would you...

GÉZA: I'm like, like, God, like, the Jesus, like, Saint Peter, I'm the controller, I've got the button right in my hands, right in my hands, red to stop, green to start, red, green, red, green...

LACI: Just like a god, you start it, you stop it.

GÉZA: I am, Uncle Laci, like a god.

LACI: For definite, but only if something happens, yeah, Géza, only if something happens…

GÉZA: I know, Uncle Laci, I know how to do it, if there's trouble, only if there's trouble, Uncle Laci.

ONE : FOURTEEN

RÓZSIKA is in the kitchen as GÉZA arrives home.

GÉZA: I'm home, Mum, home.

RÓZSIKA: I can see that, little one, I can see that. So, did anything happen today?

GÉZA: Nothing, again nothing, I've been sitting in my seat all day all week and nothing ever happens. Never…

RÓZSIKA: It's good if there's no accident, it's good, isn't it?

GÉZA: But it's not good because nothing happens, nothing, nothing happens.

RÓZSIKA: That's lucky, it's good if nothing happens.

GÉZA: What am I there for if nothing happens, why am I sitting there, what are the buttons in my hands for, Mum, what do I do with the buttons then?

RÓZSIKA: It's your job, that's why you're there, that's why they pay you, to sit there, stop the belt if something happens, Uncle Laci said that's why you're there, Uncle Laci told you, you've got the button in your hands so you can press if something happens.

GÉZA: But nothing happens, Mum, nothing happens, there's no need to stop the belt, I don't need to stop it ever, I've been at the quarry six months and I never need to stop the belt. I thought I'd need to stop the belt. I thought something's going to happen and I grab the controls and press red, I press it right, the red one. And when I press the button, the belt (*Imitates pressing.*) stops right there, and the stones jolt a bit like on the bus when Mister Karesz does the brakes, like people on the bus when Mister Karesz does it. What am I there for if the belt never stops, why do I need buttons in my hands, what for if never...

RÓZSIKA: But you must watch in case anything happens, yes, and you haven't stopped it because nothing's happened, that's the only reason. Uncle Laci, don't worry, Uncle Laci knows you know what to do, Uncle Laci knows you'd stop the belt straight off if needed, straight off you...

GÉZA: It doesn't matter what Uncle Laci knows because nothing happens, and I don't stop the belt, I'm just watching. I'm just watching like this (*imitates watching*), like watching the kitchen floor, I'm watching in the morning and after lunch too, I'm always just watching.

RÓZSIKA: Why, what do other people do, other people don't do anything else just the same thing all day...

GÉZA: But I do nothing, I don't press the button, I can't do the pressing. What do I need the button for, what for if I can't stop the belt? It's not a job to keep watching from morning, watching till evening, it's not a job because I do nothing.

GÉZA gets up and is about to leave.

RÓZSIKA: Where you going?

GÉZA: I'm going to the pub, Uncle Lajos and his lot are still there.

RÓZSIKA: What you going for this late after dinner, what for, you've never been this late...

GÉZA: What am I supposed to do at home, there's nothing on telly, nothing going happening on telly... I'd rather go to them, go to Uncle Lajos and his lot.

RÓZSIKA: But you could get to sleep early, recharge yourself, get a good sleep.

GÉZA: All day I do nothing and sit and do nothing, why do I need to recharge myself, if I do nothing?

GÉZA goes, slamming the door as he leaves.

ONE : FIFTEEN

The usual group of people are in the pub. Everyone is pretty drunk.

KARESZ: (*Calls in through the door.*) Lajos, the wife says go home because something needs mending, the pig kicked the side out of the sty or some shit...

BANDA: The wife shouldn't send me messages, she shouldn't, because then I'm for definite not going home, that's for definite. (*Pause.*) Anyhows, pig should nail it back, after all he kicked it out, nothing to do with me...

KREKÁCS: You go home, Lajos, you nail the sty and then you nail the wife, what's the matter with you, why not...

BANDA: You go home, stop fucking with me, you go home and fuck. And we'll be peeping through the window...

HERDA: Lajos, in the dark every woman looks the same, right?

Guffawing.

BANDA: Except yours is darker because her legs are as hairy as Uncle Sanyi's arsehole...

HERDA: Makes no difference anyhows what we do, I won't remember anything by morning, couldn't even tell you the last time me and the wife did it.

KREKÁCS: What, have you ever done it?

HERDA: Some time for definite, some time, but I don't know when, that I just don't know.

BANDA: Lucky you!

HERDA: What's good luck?

BANDA: That you don't remember, just that.

HERDA: Why's it good luck not to remember?

BANDA: Because then one forgets what's happened to himself, don't you?

HERDA: But why's it good if one forgets it all?

BANDA: Because it means one doesn't remember, see, it makes life worth living, see, to forget what's happened.

KREKÁCS: And one must drink so as not to be bored while forgetting, yeah, letting the time drift past, that's why.

HERDA: But what was it Lajos said, with nailing the sty and his wife, Lajos, I don't remember, what was that?

The door opens, GÉZA comes in.

KREKÁCS: Hold up, Géza's here.

GÉZA: Good evening, Uncle Lajos, good evening, Uncle Pityu, I've come by, I've come by again.

BANDA: All right, Géza, if you've come by, you've come by, have some squash now you're here.

HERDA: Not the fizzy one though, it takes the bones out of you, makes you collapse like runny shit.

All guffaw.

GÉZA: I won't have any, Uncle Lajos, I won't, I just came by, I came by, Uncle Lajos.

BANDA: Come on in, come on, what you standing there for, face all fucking miserable, what the hell's up with you?

GÉZA says nothing, just stands there.

HERDA: The kid's got a problem, can't you see, he's got a problem.

GÉZA: I'm not going tomorrow, I'm not going to work tomorrow, I don't want to, it's not real work what I'm doing, I won't go...

BANDA: What the hell's wrong with you, Géza, you been drinking, or...

KREKÁCS: Vizike got him, she got Géza!

HERDA: Shut your face, Béla, fuck you, shut it or I'll knock your teeth out.

BANDA: What's up, kid, tell us, what's up?

GÉZA: I'm not going to work, I'm not, goodbye, I'm not going...

GÉZA tries to go but HERDA grabs him.

HERDA: What you saying, what the fuck's the problem, don't you like us then or what the fuck is it...

BANDA: Stop fucking with the kid, quit fucking about with him. You can see he's got a problem, you can see that. He's not your wife, do whatever you like to her, all right, he's not your wife.

GÉZA: I'm not going, Uncle Pityu, Uncle Lajos, I'm not going, I'm not going to work tomorrow.

BANDA: Don't do this, Géza, don't do it, what's wrong, tell us, what's wrong?

GÉZA: It's no real work, Uncle Lajos, it's no real work what I'm doing.

BANDA: But you've got it down, what you do, you've got it down perfect.

GÉZA: I'm not doing anything, nothing, I'm just sitting watching stones, but I'm not doing anything...

BANDA: Well, that's exactly what you do, you sit and watch the stones.

HERDA: It's just that kind of job, you sit and watch the stones...

GÉZA: But I do nothing, I'm sitting doing nothing from morning to evening doing nothing. I've got the red and the green button and I do nothing, I don't press because nothing happens. I'm just sitting watching the stones...

BANDA: Well, the job is that you sit and watch the stones.

GÉZA: But if I never have to press then what am I sitting there for, then why am I watching the stones if I never need to press, then I got no purpose because I never need to press the button, never.

BANDA: Listen, Géza, you're like God, didn't I tell you, just like him, yeah, but you can't just go pressing willy-nilly.

HERDA: You can't just go pressing willy-nilly, just like that.

GÉZA: I can't ever press it, it's in my hands for no reason, not ever. It's not a job, it's not something to do, there's nothing to do, I'm just sitting watching stones, all day long with my eyes on the grey stones. They mix in with the black belt, and I play, like, guess when the belt's going to show between the stones, I play that from morning till evening, guess when the piles are higher, when are they lower, just watching for that, when can you see the belt, when's it going to show between the stones, but I never stop it because nothing ever happens, it's not a job, I'm just sitting there, eyes peeled and doing nothing...

BANDA: Listen, Géza, now, would it be good if you had to press it, would you like that?

GÉZA: That's why they sat me there, Uncle Lajos, to press it, that's why.

BANDA: Listen, Géza, listen, now, would you like it if you had to press it because I'm lying there on the belt all covered in blood, on the stones, would you like that?

GÉZA: But that's why I'm there, so I push it if something's up, that's why I'm there, Uncle Lajos, that's why.

BANDA: Don't you get it, Géza, don't you get it? Would you like it if I got injured, or if Pityu Herda got injured, would that be good, then you'd be happy because at last you'd get to press it, would you like that then?

GÉZA: Not that, Uncle Lajos, not that, I don't want that, I just want to press it.

BANDA: See, Géza, see, till now you've not got the whole thing that that's exactly why you're there, so pressing isn't needed.

HERDA: See, kid, see, if pressing is needed then it's big deep shit, yeah, it's curtains for someone...

KREKÁCS: Death, Géza, it's death!

GÉZA: But Uncle Lajos, if I don't sit there nothing happens anyhows, if no-one's there, still nothing happens, even then, because pressing isn't needed, it's never needed. What happens happens, even if there's no-one around, so nothing happens anyhows.

HERDA: Listen, Géza, have you thought what'd happen if there's a problem?

GÉZA: But there's not been any problems, there's not been any problems, that's the problem that there's never been anything because nothing's ever happened, and I haven't pressed the button, and if I'm not there it's just the same as now when I am sitting there.

HERDA: The kid don't get it, he doesn't get it, Jesus fuck!

KREKÁCS: Death, the kid needs death, death!

HERDA: Shut your face now, Béla! Lajos, tell him because he don't get it, the kid don't get it!

KREKÁCS: The kid needs blood, blood!

HERDA: Shut it or I'll boot your teeth out!

BANDA: Listen, Géza, if I go and fall on the belt, can you see the belt now, can you see it now?

GÉZA: (*Staring.*) I can see it, Uncle Lajos, I can see it!

BANDA: You can see me tripping on a stone and falling on the belt and the belt starts taking me too, yeah, right before your eyes, that's where the belt's dragging me off...

GÉZA: Then me, then I must press red, I press it!

BANDA: You get it now, when you see me, then you press the red and the belt stops, see, and I'll have no trouble, see, nothing.

GÉZA: But I never needed to press, Uncle Lajos, never needed to, and it makes no difference I'm there if I don't need to.

HERDA: But if one time you do, yeah, if one time, then you can save a life!

BANDA: See, Géza, my life's in your hands, and Pityu's too, see! If I fall on it, and if nobody stops it, then I'm a gonner. See, you can save a life!

GÉZA: Life, I save life, I know, Uncle Lajos, life...

KREKÁCS: You're a lifesaver, Géza, a lifesaver!

BANDA: The reason I stay alive is you pressing the red button, yeah?

HERDA: Leave him alone, he gets it, can't you see, he gets it.

BANDA: Let me speak, why do you ram your nose in, every time I open my mouth?

HERDA: I'm just saying, now he gets it.

BANDA: Of course he gets it, I told him, that's why he gets it.

HERDA: That's what I'm saying, that you told him.

BANDA: Fine, but don't say it, gets on my nerves.

KREKÁCS: Géza needs death, he needs death!

BANDA: (*To KREKÁCS.*) Drink, fuck you, don't bark!

GÉZA: I get it, I get it...

BANDA: See? He gets it.

HERDA: That's all I'm saying, he gets it.

GÉZA: See you tomorrow at the bus then, Uncle Lajos!

BANDA: All right, Géza, see you tomorrow.

GÉZA goes. BANDA suddenly shudders.

What the fuck is under the table? *(Looks under table.)*
That's not the bottle, fuck you, that's not the bottle. What the fuck you doing under the table...? It's Vizike under the table.

KREKÁCS: It's Vizike, under the table!

HERDA: When did she slide in?

KREKÁCS: I don't know.

HERDA: She been here all day?

KREKÁCS: I don't know.

HERDA: Maybe must have been yesterday she came in...

BANDA: Get your face away from there! (*Kicking.*) I'll piss in your mouth...

KREKÁCS: What's up, has the fish got caught on the maggot?

VIZIKE: (*Staggering up.*) Am I still here?

KREKÁCS: Why, where do you think, America?

VIZIKE: Has my glass been right here all along?

HERDA: Right here, glass is right here, such a good pub.

KREKÁCS: Got to put it right there else we forget where it is, this is it.

VIZIKE: Forgets, so what?

HERDA: But if we put it right there, where it was, then we'll find it if we put it right there.

VIZIKE: What if we don't know that we put it there?

KREKÁCS: Then we die, we must be dead if we don't know that, either dead, about to die or dying, but we are dead.

BANDA: What you looking at, Pityu, what you looking at on the wall, what's there?

KREKÁCS: Pityu stares through the wall, stares completely through.

HERDA: I just got Géza in my head, must be so bad for him, he's just watching the stones morning till evening...

What happiness is there for Géza, what happiness for
him, I don't know, why's Géza around, I don't know,
what he lives for if there's no enjoyment, there's no
enjoyment for him, for Géza.

BANDA: Hundred for Géza, Pityu, put money in too for
Géza...

VIZIKE: I'm needed too, am I, me too?!

HERDA: We're collecting for you, fuck you, it's for you!

KREKÁCS: I'm giving another hundred.

BANDA: Three hundred! (*Calls under table.*) Three hundred
for Géza!

HERDA: She's not there any more, Lajos.

BANDA: Where is she then, where is she?

KREKÁCS: Here, right in front of you.

BANDA: All right, I couldn't see her, she was there before,
just now. So, three hundred.

VIZIKE: Just put it in my hands. Just put it here, Lajos dear.
Three hundred's enough for Géza, just enough. I'll do it
tomorrow, just put it there, Lajos dear...

BANDA: Only after.

VIZIKE: Why you cocking me about like this, Lajos, what
you cocking me about like this for?

BANDA: So you don't get so shit-faced you forget what
you're supposed to do, and it doesn't happen. Tomorrow,
yeah, from the pub...

KREKÁCS: I'd like to see, that Géza, what he does, I'd like
to see that for definite. And, like, how big he's got, I'd
like to see that.

BANDA: Come on, Pityu, let's go.

BANDA and HERDA are heading home.

HERDA: What are these fucking dogs barking for, why they barking all day?

BANDA: It's their job, yeah, they're supposed to do that.

HERDA: Must feel like shit being a dog, must feel like pure shit.

BANDA: Why would it feel like shit, all you've got to do is bark all day, yeah, you're barking and that's it, they're supposed to bark.

HERDA: But they're splitting my head, my head is totally splitting. Look at the pavement, look at it, can you see that?

BANDA: See what, see what, course I can see.

HERDA: Not, like, can you see, no, the pavement, can you see the pavement?

BANDA: Course I can see that, why couldn't I see that?

HERDA: But, like, look, as we're walking, look, like the stones on the belt, see, when you take a step it's like the stones on the belt.

BANDA: Right, yeah, just like that, exactly like that.

HERDA: Like what?

BANDA: Like the stones on the belt, like that.

HERDA: What stones?

BANDA: I don't know.

End of Part One.

TWO : ONE

The bedroom at dawn. The alarm clock doesn't ring because RÓZSIKA clicks it off.

RÓZSIKA: Wake up, Géza, it's almost five, wake up!

GÉZA: I didn't hear it ring, it didn't ring, I didn't hear it, I wake up when it rings, I put on my trousers, socks, shoes, go to the kitchen, breakfast, food in the bag, "What am I taking today, Mum, what is it?" Mum says I'm taking bread and butter, bread and butter, and I tell Mum, "Yes, bread and butter, and sausage on the side, Mum, will I have sausage on the side too?" "Yes, there'll be sausage on the side too." It didn't ring, I didn't hear it ring, I sleep until it rings, just till then, till then I'm in bed, then I'm awake, I'm either awake or asleep, and when it rings I don't ask questions, I don't say that I have something else to do, when it rings I get up, when it doesn't ring I'm asleep, in bed, when I'm asleep I don't say, "Why aren't I awake?" and when I've got to be awake I don't say, "Why aren't I sleeping?" I don't ask questions like that, like this should be and that should be, because I know that when the alarm rings, this and that needs to happen, but this time it didn't ring, I didn't hear it ring, what am I supposed to do now, should I stay in bed, or should I get up, it didn't ring…

RÓZSIKA: I woke up just before, I turned the alarm off.

GÉZA: Did Mum turn it off?

RÓZSIKA: Yes.

GÉZA: Mum turned the button of the alarm off.

RÓZSIKA: I turned it off, I thought I'd wake you…

GÉZA: But Mum can't ring.

RÓZSIKA: No.

GÉZA: Mum can't, only the alarm can, but it isn't ringing now, not ringing, the alarm isn't ringing now...

RÓZSIKA switches the alarm on.

That's it, now it's ringing, wake-up time, I know it's wake-up time, I know that.

RÓZSIKA: Wake up, little one, I'm making breakfast, get dressed, I'm going to the kitchen.

GÉZA: Yes, Mum, yes. (*Getting dressed by lamplight.*)

RÓZSIKA: So dark it is, so much darkness, even though it's spring already.

TWO : TWO

The street at dawn. GÉZA is going to work.

MAN: You going to the quarry, Géza?

GÉZA: I'm going, Uncle Jani, I've got to go, so Uncle Lajos gets no trouble, and Uncle Pityu Herda.

MAN: Good on you, Géza, things need watching, don't they?

GÉZA: Got to watch, yeah, got to watch close. I watch the belt, I watch the stones to see if they go properly on the belt, then if Uncle Lajos falls on it, I stop it so Uncle Lajos gets no trouble.

HERDA: (*Shouts.*) Hurry up, Géza, don't miss the bus...

GÉZA: Jumbo stupid dogs you've got, Uncle Jani, jumbo stupid barking dogs you've got.

MAN: Someone's got to watch the house all day, case someone wants to break in, see?

GÉZA: I see, got to watch, anyhows I'm not scared of them, they're jumbo stupid dogs, I'm not scared, they're tied up, woof-woof, got to be stupid doing that all day at full volume, really stupid, woof-woof. (*Approaches the bus stop.*)

HERDA: Come on, Géza, come on, kid!

GÉZA: I'm coming... I was just looking at the dogs, and how much they bark, that's what I was looking at, woof-woof, so much. (*Arrives at the bus stop.*)

BANDA: See, it's good to be here, yeah, it's good.

GÉZA: It's good to be here, Uncle Lajos has been waiting for me, it's good to be here, and Uncle Pityu has been waiting for me too.

BANDA: What you got for snack?

BANDA pats GÉZA on the back. GÉZA is surprised, but then he smiles.

GÉZA: Bread and butter with sausage.

BANDA: That's good, that's very good.

GÉZA: What did Aunty Ilonka pack for Uncle Lajos?

BANDA: Lard and bread.

GÉZA: That's good, Uncle Lajos, that's very good. (*Pause.*) Does Uncle Lajos always eat the same, always?

BANDA: Always.

GÉZA: Why does Uncle Lajos always eat the same thing?

BANDA: I don't know, Géza, I don't know why.

HERDA: Here comes Karesz!

The bus can be heard arriving.

TWO : THREE

Afternoon. On the bus, homeward bound.

HERDA: Géza was a king today, what a king.

BANDA: God, like a god.

GÉZA: King, god, king, that was me today, that was me, Uncle Lajos, that was me.

BANDA: Like the dog at home, yeah!

GÉZA: I see, the dog, like the dog... How like the dog?

BANDA: If it wasn't there, yeah, everything would get ransacked, nothing left for us... See, just like them, all day long they're watching, and night time too, see?

GÉZA: I'm like the dogs, they're gods too, the dogs, all day they go woof-woof, and night time too, woof-woof.

HERDA: For definite, they go like that all day, because it's their job to go like that.

GÉZA: Like I watch the belt all day, all day they go woof-woof, like me and the belt, kings, gods, dog-gods...

HERDA: Leave it, kid, leave it, you get it all right, you ain't that stupid.

GÉZA: I'm not that stupid, like those dogs, I'm not stupid like them, I just pretend, like them, but I'm not stupid.

TWO : FOUR

Evening in the pub.

HERDA: Anyhows, that fucking winter's gone.

KREKÁCS: Gone, the son of a whore, finally gone.

BANDA: I've plugged the fridge back in.

HERDA: What, you unplugged it?

BANDA: For definite, I unplugged it for winter, what kind of idiot heats the kitchen, yeah, burns six hundred weight of wood, then starts freezing up one of the corners, right, that person's totally stupid.

KREKÁCS: That person is totally stupid, for definite, totally stupid.

BANDA: Now I've plugged it.

HERDA: What have you plugged, what you talking about?

BANDA: I'm saying, the fridge.

HERDA: Oh, that.

BANDA: Yes, that.

HERDA: I thought something else.

BANDA: Do you want me to laugh now?

HERDA: At what?

BANDA: Doesn't matter.

KREKÁCS: The kid's very silent today.

HERDA: What, is the kid still around, you still here, Géza?

GÉZA: I'm still here, Uncle Pityu, I'm here, I'm being silent here, Uncle Pityu, here.

BANDA: All right, enough for today, go home now.

GÉZA: All right, all right, got to go, I know, got to go.

HERDA: Well, go then, don't just say it, go!

GÉZA: I'm going, Uncle Pityu, going now, well, tomorrow then, Uncle Lajos, tomorrow then.

BANDA: All right, Géza, bye then.

GÉZA is leaving.

HERDA: (*To VIZIKE.*) So, do what you're supposed to, go after him.

VIZIKE: All right, stop pushing me, I'm going. Wait, Géza, hang on, listen, I'm going that way too, I've had enough of stupid Lajos too, and Uncle Pityu, I've totally had enough too.

GÉZA: I'm listening, okay, I'm listening, let's go together, okay.

They start to leave.

VIZIKE: Least you're not going on your own, yeah?

GÉZA: I'm not going on my own, at least it's good I'm not going on my own.

GÉZA and VIZIKE go out of the pub. In the street...

VIZIKE: What are those dumb animals barking for?

GÉZA: They're barking because they're dogs, their job's to be dogs.

VIZIKE: They shouldn't bark every night, shouldn't every time I come along.

GÉZA: They're meant to. The kings are barking, the dog-gods, it's them barking, the dog-gods, it's them!

VIZIKE: What is it, Géza, just...stop it, all right!

GÉZA: Woof-woof-woof, the gods are barking, there are gods in the sky, in the sky and they bark woof-woof-woof...

VIZIKE: Quit talking shit, Géza, about the gods, quit talking shit.

GÉZA: They don't turn off the button, in the sky they don't, they're not meant to turn it off, yeah.

VIZIKE: Well, this is me, I'm home, Géza.

GÉZA: I keep going, I'm not home yet, I keep going.

VIZIKE: There's not any dogs at my place, look, there's not.

GÉZA: There's not, there's no gods here, there's not, they're not barking woof-woof-woof.

VIZIKE: Come in, I'll give you something, I'll give you bread and butter, yeah, bread and butter.

GÉZA: It's not possible, got to go, Mum's waiting for me, Mum's waiting.

VIZIKE: (*Dragging GÉZA slightly.*) Come on, she's not waiting, she's not waiting yet, it's not seven yet, she's not waiting yet. (*Opens door, pulling GÉZA inside.*)

GÉZA: Why should I go in...? (*Taking small steps inside.*) What do I want in there, I don't know what I want in there, I don't know.

VIZIKE: Bread and butter, good bread and butter!

GÉZA: The alarm doesn't ring, it doesn't ring, I'm not going, the alarm doesn't ring! (*Stopping, going, stopping, going.*)

VIZIKE: I'll ring it, kid, I'll ring it, don't you worry!

VIZIKE drags GÉZA in and pushes him onto a sofa.

GÉZA: What does Aunty Vizike want, what do you want?!

VIZIKE: Got to take these off, can't do it otherwise, yeah, got to take these off!

She unbuttons GÉZA's clothes.

GÉZA: Aunty Vizike, I mustn't! (*Yelling.*) I mustn't!

VIZIKE: (*Trying to shove GÉZA's hand between her legs.*) Touch here, Géza, come on, touch here!

GÉZA: I know what you want, I know, but the doctor said I mustn't, she said I mustn't in Vác. (*Pushes VIZIKE away roughly.*) She said I mustn't, all right, not me.

VIZIKE is hurled against the wardrobe. There is blood.

VIZIKE: (*Screams.*) Have you gone stupid, Géza, have you gone totally stupid?!

GÉZA: She said I mustn't, all right, she said I mustn't.

VIZIKE: (*Squeals.*) You're stupid, Géza, totally stupid.

GÉZA: I'm going home, I'm running home now. There are no dogs. There are no dogs here.

GÉZA runs away. VIZIKE stays, wiping her forehead.

VIZIKE: God, god!

TWO : FIVE

At home.

GÉZA: Good evening to you, Mum, I'm home, good evening.

RÓZSIKA: What happened? What's up with you? The look on your face!

GÉZA: Nothing, I just watched the stones all day.

RÓZSIKA: I can see there's something.

GÉZA: What can Mum see, what can you see? She can't see nothing, I was just watching the stones, like the dogs watch the house, like they guard the house so that nothing bad happens to Uncle Pityu Herda and Uncle Lajos Banda.

RÓZSIKA: You're a proper worker, like your father, just like he was too.

GÉZA: I work proper, I get up every day, I go to work, I watch the stone, I come home, I go to bed, the alarm rings, I get up again, every day, but if I don't go the belt is still there, and the stones, it's still there anyhows, Mum.

RÓZSIKA: But if there's trouble, it's you that presses the button, you stop it if something happens, like, if Uncle Pityu falls on the belt.

GÉZA: There wasn't any trouble, Mum, there wasn't. And there won't be any tomorrow, Mum, there won't be any tomorrow either, there's never been trouble, there wasn't and there won't be.

RÓZSIKA: It's lucky that there's not been trouble. That's just what you need, for there to be an accident, just what you need.

GÉZA: You don't get it, Mum, you don't get it. If there's no trouble, why am I there?

RÓZSIKA: To press the red button when there's trouble, that's why, didn't Uncle Laci say you watch in case you need to press the red button…

GÉZA: There's no point in pressing the red button if I'm not allowed to press the red button, no point. (*Getting more agitated.*) I'm sitting, Mum, I'm sitting watching the belt go, I'm watching it, but I'm not doing anything, I'm just watching as the belt goes past, it goes in the morning, goes an hour later, and later on it's still going, but there's no point me being there, if I'm not there it goes anyhows, even then.

RÓZSIKA: Come on, have some food, eat something!

GÉZA: I don't need it, Mum, I don't need it now, my tummy's all upset, Mum, really upset. (*Banging with his hands.*) Nothing happens, nothing! (*He yells.*) I do nothing! (*He writhes.*) I just watch and nothing.

Suddenly, he becomes quiet and staring out blankly. His mum comforts him.

TWO : SIX

The pub. All of the regulars are there. The door opens and VIZIKE comes in.

KREKÁCS: Well fucking hell, Vizike's here!

VIZIKE: Lajos, give me the three hundred!

BANDA: Tell us first, your royal highness, tell us!

HERDA: What happened?

KREKÁCS: How big the kid got, I hear fools have got them big as horses.

BANDA: Shut your trap, Béla. So?

VIZIKE: Well…

BANDA: What do you mean, well?

VIZIKE: Well, I mean that Géza…

BANDA: Don't quack like a duck, don't quack! What happened, tell us, what happened?

VIZIKE: But I'm telling you what happened, why do you always butt yourself in, I'm just telling you that.

BANDA: Never mind what I'm doing, what you did with Géza, tell us about that.

VIZIKE: That's what I'm doing, fuck's sake, I'd tell you all about it if you'd shut your fucking cakehole. Where's the money, anyhows?

BANDA: We've got the money all right, all there, don't you worry about that. So what happened?

VIZIKE: So nothing happened.

KREKÁCS: Nothing? Shit a brick sideways, didn't anything happen?

BANDA: How come nothing happened, what the hell you going on about, what the hell? We told you what to do, didn't we?

VIZIKE: You told me but nothing happened, nothing doing, the kid ran off, all right, he ran off.

BANDA: How the fuck did he run off, how the fuck could he run off?

VIZIKE: What you yelling for, can't you see the cut on my head, got blood all over my hair too, what you yelling for? He shoved me against the wardrobe and ran off, all right, he ran off. But the money's owed me because I did what I could...

HERDA: What money?

VIZIKE: I did what I was meant!

BANDA: Money! Money! You know what's owed to you, you know what? That I'm going to give your arse the boot!

BANDA pushes VIZIKE away. She loses her balance and touches her head.

VIZIKE: (*Screams.*) Now you come at me, isn't it enough Géza came at me, isn't that enough?

BANDA: (*Shaking her.*) Géza doesn't hurt anybody, get it, Géza doesn't hurt, Géza loves everyone, Géza's a god compared to you, all right, a god, what the fuck did you do to him, what the fuck, you animal!

HERDA: (*Trying to separate them.*) Leave her alone, Lajos, leave her, not her fault!

BANDA: Leave her, why leave her, Vizike's dumb as a table-leg! She attacked the kid, for definite, she attacked him. She doesn't know the kid still don't know what to do. The idiot attacked him so the kid got scared, when has he ever shoved somebody, he's innocent as a kicked-off pair of old boots, you can only stumble over him…

VIZIKE: I'm not a nurse, I've only got my cunt, yeah, that's what I gave him, I can't give him nothing else, all right, I'm not a nurse!

BANDA: You are stupid, fuck you, really stupid, problem is you don't know what you've done, that's how stupid you are.

HERDA: Leave her alone now, Lajos. Whole thing was your idea, wasn't it yours? Leave her alone now.

BANDA: But I didn't mean it this way, not like this! What's this piss-cunt done, this piss-brain, what's she done?!

KREKÁCS: Well, that is yet to be revealed.

HERDA: What is yet to be revealed?

KREKÁCS: Well, that is.

BANDA: What?

KREKÁCS: How big.

HERDA: How big what is?

BANDA: What do you mean, how big?

KREKÁCS: Has he got one as big as a horse's?

BANDA: What?

HERDA: A horse's?

KREKÁCS: A horse's.

BANDA: I don't know.

KREKÁCS: Well, Vizike don't know neither.

HERDA: For definite she don't, she doesn't know anything.

BANDA: Nothing, she's so stupid.

KREKÁCS: But you don't know neither.

BANDA: We don't.

HERDA: Or anyhows, if we did, we forgot.

KREKÁCS: Forgot what?

HERDA: I don't know.

TWO : SEVEN

Morning in the street.

MAN: Hello, Rózsika.

RÓZSIKA: Morning. You're up very early.

WOMAN: Isn't the kid bored of stone watching?

RÓZSIKA: Well, that's his job, and if something happens and he's not there, there could be a death. Géza knows the importance of it.

MAN: No small thing to watch the belt, all the stones shaking on it, all day long. It's like when the telly goes fuzzy like it's full of ants.

RÓZSIKA: Even Géza needs something to do, and he knows how to do this. And it's good for the German because Géza's faulty, so he doesn't need to pay as much.

WOMAN: Do you know how much he gets?

RÓZSIKA: Not much, just a bit, but that's something anyhows, that he gets anything. Well, I'm going. These dogs don't half bark, they still don't recognise me, they think I'm a stranger.

MAN: They're meant to watch, yeah.

RÓZSIKA: Fine, but after all this time you'd think they'd recognise me.

MAN: Point is they bark, better they bark at everyone than no-one, yeah.

RÓZSIKA: I suppose that's true.

RÓZSIKA starts to leave.

WOMAN: (*Calling after RÓZSIKA.*) Anyhows, how much, Rózsika, how much does the German pay?

RÓZSIKA: The German needs him, that's for definite.

WOMAN: But how much?

RÓZSIKA: Because of the insurance, so he don't have to pay.

RÓZSIKA is gone.

MAN: What do you care about the money, why do you want to know so much, huh?

WOMAN: I was just curious, how much he gives for that.

MAN: What do you mean, for that?

WOMAN: After all, he's doing nothing, just sitting and watching, how can you earn money sitting down, just sitting!

MAN: It's a job like that.

WOMAN: Earning money though, as opposed to you.

MAN: I tried.

WOMAN: You've been nothing your whole life. Even the kid's better than you. You don't even exist, not even compared to that idiot kid. You never had money, never.

MAN: I haven't because of you, because you couldn't save up, you could never manage money.

WOMAN: Manage what, what you brought home, what was that, how much was that, how much do you think Jani Vajsz or Béla Szabó brought home, you reckon same as you, is that what you think?

MAN: Just the same, except it was enough for them, just about enough, but you could never manage money.

WOMAN: Double, best it's me that tells you, they took home double what you did, you've achieved nothing all your life. Anyhows, what's the point in saying it now, there's no point.

MAN: Why did I stick with you, if I only I knew, why?! On account of the kids, only on account of the kids, but I'll leave one day, either that or I'll do you in.

WOMAN: You're such a coward, such a coward, you wouldn't dare do anything, you're a coward and a shithead.

MAN: One day I'll do you in, one day I'll pay you back for everything, one day, you wait. And leave Géza out of it, Géza's a god compared to you, a god. That kid loves everyone, even you.

TWO : EIGHT

Morning in the shop.

RÓZSIKA: Hello, Marika, hello.

MARIKA: Morning, Aunty Rózsika. Is Géza still keen on the job?

RÓZSIKA: Well, he goes every day.

MARIKA: I see him every morning, punctual as clockwork…

RÓZSIKA: Oh, for definite, he couldn't be late.

MARIKA: When we went to school, even then, soon as the bell rang he took his books and packed up, didn't matter the teacher was still in the room. "I'm not finished, Géza," "The bell rang, Sir, finished, the bell rang, Sir's supposed to leave, supposed to leave now," "But I'm not finished, Géza," "It's not Sir to finish, it's the bell."

They laugh.

RÓZSIKA: After all, he was right, wasn't he?

MARIKA: Well, yes, the teacher felt he had to go, sometimes couldn't even give us homework neither. That's why we loved Géza so much, when he was around they couldn't keep the class back.

RÓZSIKA: Well, Géza for definite can be loved, can't he?

MARIKA: For definite. Because Géza loves everyone too.

RÓZSIKA: He loves everyone, that's for definite.

MARIKA: It's difficult with a kid like that, Aunty Rózsika, it's very difficult, mine are healthy but they still take up all my time, don't hate me but they do, they take it all up.

RÓZSIKA: What should I do, Marika, I often think it but I don't dare say it, like, why did I get this affliction on me, but I never dare say it.

MARIKA: I know, Aunty Rózsika, I know.

RÓZSIKA: But then I get used to it, this is what I got. And now I miss him, and the day's so empty when he's not home, I go and feed the pigs, then I even talk to myself,

I talk to the pigs, Marika, because I miss the kid during the day, and I'm scared something bad might happen to him, that's what I'm scared of.

MARIKA: There won't be any trouble, Aunty Rózsika, there won't be any. Géza knows the drill, he knows how it all works, what to do when, he knows it all.

RÓZSIKA: When I'm dead he'll be on his own anyhows. On his own.

TWO : NINE

Daytime. By the conveyor belt.

LACI: We're stopping! Lunchtime!

BANDA: So, how's your bread and butter?

GÉZA: Bread and butter with sausage, I like bread and butter with sausage, Uncle Lajos.

BANDA: Not asking any questions, Géza?

GÉZA: What should I ask, Uncle Lajos?

BANDA: Like, how the lard is, something like that.

GÉZA: I'll be quiet, Uncle Lajos.

HERDA: What are you being quiet for?

BANDA: What's the problem, Géza?

GÉZA: There isn't a problem, Uncle Lajos.

HERDA: Because of Vizike, yeah?

BANDA: She came at you, that's the problem, she came at you...

GÉZA: That didn't cause problems, Uncle Lajos, it didn't, because I ran away, Uncle Lajos, I ran away, because the doctor says I mustn't, not meant to, so I ran away because I mustn't and it didn't cause problems, Uncle Lajos.

They keep eating without talking.

BANDA: Pityu, say something to the kid, will you?

HERDA: Say what? Anyhows, I don't feel like talking about nothing now either.

BANDA: Did anything happen at home or what? The wife?

HERDA: I don't care about that, I don't care about the wife.

BANDA: What then?

HERDA: Nothing, just Sanyi Czeher got put in hospital because his liver swelled.

BANDA: It'll squash down in the hospital, won't it?

HERDA: Or he'll die, like Jani Bárdi last year, and Karesz Kovács in the summer, and the rest of them, they've already croaked. Jani was in my year at school, Karesz was a year older.

BANDA: You're stupid, Pityu, don't shit yourself so much.

HERDA: But I shat myself because I've had liver problems before, yeah, I've had it…

BANDA: Look, we ain't even going to notice when we die, we're not going to feel nothing. What did Uncle Imre Rák say when he had a heart attack, what did he say?

HERDA: I don't know, what did he say?

BANDA: That the whole thing is like you're floating up into the skies, everything gets dead light and you don't care about anything, like drinking a fine drink, like that, and everything just gleaming all around you, just like watching a film, like that.

HERDA: Somehow, I don't feel like trying it, I just don't.

BANDA: Don't shit your load, nothing's going to happen, you can't control it anyhows, it's not like a tractor, like, I'm turning the wheel so it turns back.

HERDA: But it's not the same.

BANDA: What's not the same?

HERDA: Like when I die, it's not the same.

BANDA: That's just what I'm saying, it doesn't depend on you, all right, it either happens or not, what can you do about it?

HERDA: Booze, that's what scares me, my liver. When you've got something too, then you'll know what I'm talking about, yeah, when you get dragged into intensive care at the hospital in Vác and wake up all covered in tubes, then you'll know what I'm talking about.

BANDA: You can't think about that the whole time.

HERDA: All right, let's do some work. Come on, Géza, come on.

BANDA: Come on now, Géza, all right, we're starting, why you staring out front like a dog having a shit?

GÉZA: I don't feel like it, I don't want to, I'm going home instead.

BANDA: You're daft, Géza, don't mess us about, sit in your place, then we can start.

HERDA: Come here, Laci, come over here.

LACI: What is it now, what are you hanging about for, if the German sees this he'll fucking kill me.

HERDA: Géza doesn't want to, he says he won't, he's going home, that's what he says.

LACI: What the fuck?!

BANDA: He doesn't want to.

LACI: Géza, get up, we got discipline here, it's a workplace, no idling here! (*GÉZA gets scared.*) What do I tell the German, if he sees you're not here, what do I tell him, who's watching safety, you know what the German does to me then, know what he does, he kicks my arse out, he'll kick me out because of you, because I've not got anyone for safety!

GÉZA: Workplace, discipline, discipline, workplace, German needs safety, German doesn't want to pay, German knows how to save money, he really knows that. So what that it doesn't matter what I do, because I don't got to do anything, I'm stupid, like the dogs that bark in the yard, I'm stupid like that, woof-woof... (*He heads for his chair.*)

LACI: Leave it, Géza, I told you why you got to do it, yeah, I told you you're needed if there's trouble, yeah, that's safety, that's what the insurance told the German, that's what the German told me.

GÉZA: There hasn't been any trouble, there hasn't been any yet, why am I here, what am I for if there's no trouble, there won't be any trouble...

BANDA: You're the chief controller, Géza, yeah, you're the boss, more boss than Uncle Laci, more boss than him because only you can stop it if there's trouble.

GÉZA: The dogs are gods in the yard, dog-kings, dog-gods, stupid, stupid, stupid...

The belt starts moving. GÉZA is in his seat. BANDA and HERDA go towards the pile of stones.

BANDA: Something's got to be done with Géza.

HERDA: But what?

BANDA: I don't know.

HERDA: This is it, nothing we can do.

They exit, the sound of barking dog gets closer, an explosion, the sound of stones falling, dog howling, a crash. BANDA and HERDA can be heard shouting off stage...

Watch out, Lajos, stone's falling, watch out! God!

BANDA: I'm watching but that dumb animal ain't moving.

HERDA: Get the fuck away, get away, whose is the massive dog?

BANDA: Been hanging round for a week, it must have escaped from someone.

HERDA: Get away!

The sound of stones sliding and howling. Enter BANDA and HERDA.

HERDA: Well, it's a gonner, big stupid animal, what the hell did it stay for, what the hell for?

BANDA: Listen, Pityu, listen to me, Pityu, I've got an idea, how come I didn't think of this before, god.

HERDA: What do you want to do?

BANDA: Here is a dog, a carcass, do you get it? It's bleeding all over!

HERDA: No. I mean I get it, but what is there to get?

BANDA: That here is a dog, dead, you see? Smashed by the stone.

HERDA: It's dead, so what?

BANDA: Meaning Géza, see, meaning the belt, it could convey it, you see?

HERDA: Meaning we put the dog on the belt for Géza, is that what you want?

BANDA: Meaning you're screaming, like "Ugh, Lajos, what happened to you, ugh, Lajos," yeah, and the kid sees the dog on the belt...

HERDA: Meaning you've become a dog or what the hell? Like, the belt's got a dog on and I'm yelling, like, "Ugh, Lajos, you've become a dog," or what the hell do you want...? The kid can see it's a dog, the kid's not stupid, all right, he can see...

LACI enters and listens to BANDA.

BANDA: Look, we get the bits of dog, we roll them up in my shirt, then stick it amongst the stones all bloody, and then you scream, you get it?

HERDA: Right! That's really good, god, we'll have Géza, we'll really have him.

They cut the carcass into pieces and tear up the shirt.

BANDA: Here's my coat too, put it there so he don't see through it.

HERDA: Good, it's ready, it can go. (*They throw the dog pieces on the belt.*)

BANDA: Then I'll go then, you start!

HERDA: Good, go then, yes. (*Screaming...*) Ugh, Lajos, ugh, what's happened to you, oh god, oh god, oh god, what's happened to you?!

LACI: Géza, Géza, watch the belt, Géza!

GÉZA: I'm watching but there's nothing, there isn't!

LACI: Watch out, Géza, hasn't the belt got Lajos?

GÉZA: I can't see... There are stones with blood, and...!

HERDA: Press the button now, Géza, what are you waiting for?

GÉZA: I pressed it, I pressed it, I've pressed it, it's just the momentum that keeps it going, it's going to stop, it's going to stop, what's happened to Uncle Lajos, what's happened to Uncle Lajos?

LACI: Come down from the seat, Géza, come down!

GÉZA: I didn't do it, it wasn't me, Uncle Laci, it wasn't me, I stopped it, Uncle Laci, I did.

LACI: You're not to blame, Géza. I know that, you're not to blame at all.

GÉZA: Uncle Lajos, how did it happen, so smashed, he's blown up, Uncle Lajos has blown up or whatever he's done, Uncle Lajos.

HERDA: You stopped it well, kid, you did well but it was too late for Lajos, too late, it's not your fault. God.

GÉZA: I did, I pressed the button, I pressed it.

LACI: Go home, Géza, go home, you've done enough today, take the bus and go home, and if you want, stay at home tomorrow too if you want.

GÉZA: I'm coming tomorrow, Uncle Laci, I'm coming tomorrow, that's my job, I couldn't help it, I stopped it, I did. I'll be here tomorrow, Uncle Laci.

TWO : TEN

At home. The afternoon.

GÉZA: Good afternoon, Mum, I've come home.

RÓZSIKA: What's happened, little one, what's happened?

GÉZA: I stopped the belt, I pressed the button and stopped the belt.

RÓZSIKA: Why did you stop it, little one, why?

GÉZA: I stopped it.

RÓZSIKA: Why did you need to, little one?

GÉZA: That's my job, Mum, that's my job, that's why. I pressed the red button and the belt stopped, it stopped just fine.

RÓZSIKA: But why did you have to press it?

GÉZA: I stopped it because that's my job, but it was too late for Uncle Lajos, it was too late, for Uncle Lajos.

RÓZSIKA: Why was it too late for Uncle Lajos, what's happened?

GÉZA: Uncle Lajos was taken to pieces by the explosion.

RÓZSIKA: Was what, what happened?

GÉZA: To pieces, Mum, like the pig in winter time, like Dad used to do to the pig, like that he got taken to pieces.

RÓZSIKA: Lord Almighty, Lord Almighty, what's happened?

GÉZA: Mum, it wasn't my fault, I stopped the belt, I stopped it like I was meant to, straight away, I pressed it and the belt stopped.

RÓZSIKA: It's not your fault, of course, you couldn't help it, you knew what to do. Lord Almighty!

GÉZA: But it's finished for Uncle Lajos, completely.

RÓZSIKA: The poor man, he must have been drunk, must be why, it's not your fault he exploded, you did what you had to.

GÉZA: It wasn't the belt that took him to pieces, not the belt, the dynamite, it tore him to pieces, like meatloaf, that much.

RÓZSIKA: You did what you had to, you did. Lajos, Lord Almighty, Lajos is in pieces!

GÉZA: (*Getting more and more tormented.*) Mum, I pressed on time, he was already in pieces when he fell on the belt, I just wanted something to do, so that I'd be worthwhile watching the stones, I watch the stones all day, I just wanted to be busy, I didn't mean for trouble for Uncle Lajos, I didn't mean that, I'm going to tell Aunty Ilonka that it's not my fault, I'm going to tell her that I pressed the button, that I just wanted to work, and do something too, and sit there for a reason, but Uncle Lajos, I didn't mean for him, and probably it's better for Aunty Ilonka anyhows, because she was all angry at Uncle Lajos, that he drinks all evening in the pub and doesn't go home and fix the pig sty, it's better for Aunty Ilonka too, but it's not my fault, I kept on thinking how bad for Aunty Ilonka that Uncle Lajos didn't love her, but I'd never mean that for Uncle Lajos, because I liked him and he always asked me what I brought for snack, Uncle Lajos always asked that. I liked Uncle Lajos.

RÓZSIKA: (*Pulling GÉZA to her, calming him.*) Lie down, lie down!

GÉZA: It wasn't me, not me.

RÓZSIKA: Lie down!

GÉZA calms down a bit and lies down. Silence. All of a sudden he starts again. He becomes more tense as the scene goes on. His gestures become more and more aggressive.

GÉZA: Aunty Ilonka won't be angry at me, not my fault, I switched it off…

RÓZSIKA: Relax, relax…

More silence.

GÉZA: (*Suddenly sitting up.*) Here comes the bus, it's arriving, they're getting off and bringing the news…

RÓZSIKA: Stay now. Nobody cares about the bus. Stay!

GÉZA lies down. After a pause he starts again.

GÉZA: But I must go down to the pub, I must go there!

RÓZSIKA: No, you're not going to the pub, you're not leaving.

She calms GÉZA. He lies down again. After a short pause he jumps up.

GÉZA: I'm going to go down to them, so they won't think it's my fault, I did watch, I pressed the button.

RÓZSIKA: Stay!

GÉZA: I've got to go down, I must.

RÓZSIKA: Listen, you stay! You can't leave…doctor said that. Time like this you must relax, at a time like this…

GÉZA: Doctor told Uncle Pityu that he'd die in half a year, and Uncle Pityu's still alive, I've got to go down. (*He jumps up and heads for the door. RÓZSIKA grabs him.*)

RÓZSIKA: Stay home!

GÉZA: (*Pushing her away, just as he pushed VIZIKE.*) I've got to go down, the bus just came. I've got to go down.

GÉZA runs out of the kitchen.

TWO : ELEVEN

The pub. There is a good atmosphere.

BANDA: Then I said to Pityu let's throw the carcass on the belt, let Gézakid have something to do, so he don't think he sits there for no reason.

KREKÁCS: So then you threw it on?

BANDA: Well, we rolled up the pieces in my shirt and threw them on, blood all over the place, and Pityu was yelling like "Ugh, Lajos, what happened to you," yelling, nearly screaming his tonsils out, and of course the kid shat his pants when he sees the bloody bits of flesh, shat his pants like anything.

VIZIKE: Totally shat his pants?

HERDA: Totally shat his pants, he pressed the stop, just shivering all over, so scared he got.

BANDA: I don't believe he'll want to stop it any more.

KREKÁCS: I reckon he's best off if he doesn't have to do anything there.

BANDA: So he was just staring at the bloody pieces with his big boogly eyes...

The door opens. GÉZA enters.

...and Laci was telling him, "Go home now, Géza, go, you've done your job well."

GÉZA is standing and watching BANDA.

KREKÁCS: Lajos! (*Poking BANDA.*) Lajos, look at the door!

VIZIKE: Look, Géza's there!

BANDA: Come on, Géza, come on in!

GÉZA doesn't move.

BANDA: The whole thing was a joke, see, come on, Géza, don't hang about at the door!

GÉZA: (*Doesn't move away from the door.*) Dead, Uncle Lajos is dead, taken to pieces like the pig, Uncle Lajos is dead...

BANDA: Here I am, kid, can't you see?

GÉZA: Dead.

BANDA: The whole thing was a joke, see, Géza, don't fuck about, come here...

GÉZA: Uncle Lajos is dead, he died, he died, I'm not going there, I'm not going because Uncle Lajos isn't there. There is no Uncle Lajos.

GÉZA turns around and runs away.

TWO : TWELVE

Home. Morning.

WOMAN: So, what then, isn't Géza going to work?

RÓZSIKA: He doesn't want to any more, he doesn't want to.

WOMAN: It's better for him at home, better for definite, isn't it, Géza, it's better for you at home.

GÉZA is sat by the range, his body rocking back and forth. He stops for a while but doesn't answer.

RÓZSIKA: Everything's going to be like it used to be, everything just like that.

WOMAN: It was good like that as well, Rózsika.

RÓZSIKA: I missed him when he wasn't at home.

WOMAN: I believe that, Géza's a good kid.

RÓZSIKA: I missed him.

WOMAN leaves. The dogs are barking.

GÉZA: Mum!

RÓZSIKA: What is it, little one?

GÉZA: Mum, the bad thing with this checked floor is...

RÓZSIKA: Say it, little one, what is it?

GÉZA: Like I'm looking but I still can't decide if it's grey on black or black on grey, like which is the belt and which is the stone.

RÓZSIKA: You can't, Géza, you can't ever decide that.

GÉZA: Does God know, Mum, does he know?

RÓZSIKA: He for definite does, little one.

GÉZA: And if some fault happens?

RÓZSIKA: What fault?

GÉZA: Like, on planet Earth, some fault.

RÓZSIKA: Yes?

GÉZA: Like, does he mend it?

RÓZSIKA: I don't know, little one. (*Pause.*) Probably not.

End.

www.ingramcontent.com/pod-product-compliance
Ingram Content Group UK Ltd.
Pitfield, Milton Keynes, MK11 3LW, UK
UKHW020725280225
455688UK00012B/506